THE DISSUADERS

With kinder regards

Bill Shaw

Mar. 1979

D. W. D. SHAW

THE
DISSUADERS

Three Explanations of Religion

SCM PRESS LTD

334 00326 1

First published 1978
by SCM Press Ltd
58 Bloomsbury Street, London WC1

Printed in Great Britain by
Fletcher & Son Ltd, Norwich

In memory of
D.N.B.
and
I.M.W.

CONTENTS

INTRODUCTION

'What everybody knows'

What does it mean to take something for granted? Well, it means that you don't have to think about it, you don't have to question it, you just know. If this were not the case, if there were not a thousand and one things we could take for granted every day, or every hour for that matter, all work, all normal activity, life as we know it would come to a halt. I put on my coat to go out – and take for granted that it will remain on until I take it off, and that it will remain a coat until, through wear and tear and process of time, it wears out. I go to the door and turn the handle, taking for granted, among many other things, that the handle will unlatch the door and that the door will lead on to the street today as it did yesterday. I walk for the bus, taking for granted that the pavement is not hollow and will not crack without my first testing every step. And so on, on my way, taking for granted more and more with every step. If I did not do this, if I stopped to question, test investigate every move, every step, I would, not to put too fine a point on it, get nowhere fast.

That we take things for granted and have to take things for granted is not open to dispute. Why we take things for granted, or rather, what entitles us to take things for granted is another and much more complicated question. Experience must be a key factor here. If I have learned from experience that the door handle opens the door if I turn it clockwise, and what's more, if I find that this works not just once or occasionally but every time I try it, then for all practical purposes, I am entitled to assume or take for granted that the door will always open in this way. Well, not always. One day, a screw will come out, or the door will warp or the handle will come off and the handle won't open the door any more. So that literally it is not true that the door will always open if I turn the handle in a particular way. But that is nit-picking. For all practical purposes, I can take for granted that this is and will be so. Experience entitles me to say so.

Other things I am entitled to take for granted not because I have experienced them myself but because I have been reliably taught them, by people whose knowledge and judgment I trust. If I am lucky enough to be able to have my summer holiday abroad, I go into a travel agent's office, get him to consult his computer to find out if there is a seat available on the flight I want, and if he says yes and makes out a ticket, I am entitled to take for granted that when I turn up on the day, there will be a seat for me.[1] I do not know the travel agent from Adam, and have no clue how to operate the computers, but I have learned to trust the replies they give. I take for granted that they are accurate, and do not have to verify them for myself. So also with such limited working mathematical knowledge as I possess, and, not being a practising scientist, such scientific understanding about the laws of gravity or thermo-dynamics as I can lay claim to. I have been taught it, and until someone teaches me otherwise, I am entitled to take it for granted.

Other things, however, we take for granted not because we are entitled to do so on the grounds of experience or teaching. We simply take them for granted on the basis that everyone else does. They make up those unexamined propositions, beliefs, standards which 'everybody just knows'. Argument, demonstration is not necessary: these things may be safely and generally assumed and if you want to disagree you must be prepared to be odd man out. 'Everybody knows', in England, that cricket is a better game than baseball. 'Everybody knows', in Scotland, that football is a better game than cricket. Less trivially, in Western society, 'everybody knows' that it is better to have a good job in business with a car and as many 'perks' as the Inland Revenue will allow (even if it does mean travelling 20,000 miles a year) than just making ends meet running your own small-holding in Wales. 'Everybody knows' that a man with a Bentley is more important than a man with a mini. 'Everybody knows' that a man who spends his life in a monastery must be some kind of nut.

These things that 'everybody knows' are never examined, criticized, or rationally discussed on the basis that they might be either true or false. They are just taken for granted. Because they are not rational in the sense of having been accepted on the basis of reasoned argument or explanation, they cannot be easily dislodged. More than argument is required. Like prejudices, or rather, as prejudices, they are pre-rational. They can only be seriously queried when it can be accepted that 'everybody' need not necessarily be right or when courage comes to enable an independent line to be taken.

Among those things which 'everybody knows', in Western societies, are things religious, and what 'everybody' seems to know about them is that their irrelevance can be taken for granted. This is not to deny the existence of large minorities, of Christian and other religious believers, who know no such thing. Nor is it to deny either the importance which the Christian religion and the churches have played in the history and formation of modern Western nations, or the surface respect that is still paid to them, legally, culturally and socially. It is simply to assert that for the man in the street and the man in the motorway today it is quite possible to lead a normal, healthy and full life without any conscious interest in or experience of religion at all. According to popular wisdom, religion may well be a help to the weak or unstable or insecure, but the normal, mature person can and usually does do without it. Those who are so inclined may argue till the cows come home about whether there is or is not a God, but for the purposes of ordinary living, that question has no bearing at all on what makes the cookie crumble. In other words, in practical terms the 'presumption of atheism', which a distinguished philosopher recently felt compelled to argue for intellectually,[2] in stark contrast to the situation a hundred, or even sixty years ago, has filtered into the popular mind.

Given the place religion has occupied in the history of civilizations, this is a strange situation to have arrived at, and there have been many attempts to account for this process of secularization, as it is sometimes called.[3] It is, however, no part of the aim of this study to investigate this important topic, save in one respect. This respect can best be approached by imagining a modern representative of 'what everybody knows' about religion being asked why, given the admitted importance of religion in the past and the existence of convinced but apparently sane believers in the present, he shares the popular attitude of indifference, why he feels under no sort of obligation to investigate its claims. He will doubtless say that 'science' has disproved it. If he is then pressed to say which science has disproved it, he may well be on the spot at once and have to resort to something like: 'I don't know the details, but everyone knows that some scientist somewhere has done it.' Perhaps he can do better than that. Perhaps he will say: 'Psychology, of course. Didn't old Freud have the answer?' Or, though this is less likely, he might say: 'Philosophy, of course. Feuerbach explained it all in the nineteenth century, and the Logical Positivists did it again in the twentieth.' If he is then pressed to say in what way Freud, or Feuerbach explained it all away, and if he is shown that not all their arguments are admitted as valid by those who ought to know today, he may begin to see that things are not at all as simple as he had assumed. Of course this will not necessarily make him change his mind. It might, however, make him think about these things for the first time in a reasonable fashion, in a way which gets beyond 'what everybody knows'.

The truth is, of course, that there have been many attempts to 'explain it all away', and the purpose of this little book is to look at some of the more important, in the sense of influential, of these attempts. Sometimes, the influence which these attempts have had has been due not so much to the quality of the arguments presented as to the eminence and success of the author in some field other than the field of religion. This is certainly true of Sigmund Freud, the pioneer psychologist to whose daring researches and suggestions much of the impressive edifice of modern psychology and psychiatry is a monument. It is no wonder that people should listen to his conclusions on the nature and future of religion, and how much more convenient if they did not have to take the trouble to follow the argument. So also with Karl Marx, to whose ideas on social development, politics, and economics something like one third of the world's present population presently nominally adhere. No wonder people should accept his conclusions on how religions fitted into the past history of mankind and how, in the coming society, religion should have no place. What is worth noting is that neither Marx nor Freud claimed to be religious persons, or indeed to be experts in theology or the philosophy of religion. What seems to have happened is the not uncommon phenomenon of 'transferred authority'.

4

Because a thinker is an expert in one field, it is assumed that everything he says in any field whatever is entitled to the same respect. The authority which he has rightly earned in one field is 'transferred' to his speculations in another. It is not that the thinkers in question necessarily contrive this or even desire it. It just happens: their ideas are latched on to as allegedly providing a scientific basis for a position arrived at on other grounds. Thinkers such as Freud and Marx set great store on being 'scientific' (i.e. free of irrational superstitions) and it is only fair to them that the assumptions their successors have latched on to on the basis of their works should be subjected to rigorous 'scientific' scrutiny to see whether or not they are justified.

If the conclusion is reached that none of these attempts to 'explain religion away' was wholly successful, it is important to guard against any hint or implication that there is something bogus about the discipline these great thinkers were primarily associated with. That is to say, if, for example, Freud's attempt to explain away religion wholly in terms of psychology has to be rejected, this is in no way to be interpreted as an oblique attack on psychology as such. Such a position has not been unknown in some religious circles, but there is no justification for it forever. In any case, most psychologists as psychologists, while acknowledging the importance of much of Freud's pioneering work in their discipline, certainly do not accept all his conclusions, above all his conclusions on the subject of religion. To reject Freud on religion, therefore, is by no means to reject the discipline of psychology with which he was so intimately connected. Similarly with the other thinkers with whom we shall be dealing. To comment on their conclusions on the reality or the rationality of faith is by no means to comment on the validity of the disciplines they represent. This is important. From what has been said so far, it may seem as though what is to be attempted is a purely negative, defensive exercise. This is, however, quite definitely not the intention. There is something constructive to be gained from this exercise, and it is important that this should not be lost sight of.

The point can best be made by referring to the phenomenon of heresy in the history of the Christian church, and its relation to doctrine or the official teaching of the church. The point has often been made that heresies do not arise in a vacuum. They have a

5

definite historical setting. They arise not because someone has some crack-pot idea which finds some support and seems to threaten the faith and life of the church. They arise, much more likely, because some legitimate aspect of Christian teaching or experience has become overlooked or denied by the church. Those who care about this aspect of teaching or experience refuse to let it be denied or overlooked, and it almost seems that the only way they can effectively do this is by over-emphasizing or stressing the neglected teaching or experience to the detriment of some other legitimate aspect. The 'orthodox' or 'official' church, threatened by this new emphasis, condemns it, but in so doing is forced to take account of the protest involved in it. So, though the heresy is condemned and apparently 'dealt with', the consequence is not simply a return to the *status quo* existing before the heresy saw light. A new situation is brought into being in which account has to be taken in some measure of the overlooked aspect against which the heresy was a protest reaction in the first place.

In a similar way, the 'explanations' or reductions of religion to be considered in the following chapters did not suddenly appear on the scene, in a vacuum, as it were. They were essentially connected with new fast-developing sciences, like sociology or psychology, or they were bound up with new and total ways of looking at things, like the philosophy of Feuerbach or the theory of history which Marx provided. So, too, as with heresies, after the dust seems to be settling on controversy, there is really no going back to the situation before the dust storm was created in the first place. A new factor has been introduced which cannot be overlooked. What lies behind the explanation or reduction remains a permanent element in the data of which the student or follower of a religion fails to take account at his peril.

It is important to see that this is not simply an awkward or unfortunate fact. It is a mistake to treat the apparent wholesale attacks on religion as if they were wholly and unconditionally destructive and to be repelled as such. Even if they were sometimes by their original proponents intended to destroy (though we shall discover that they were not all intended to destroy) even then they provide an opportunity of discovering a constructive element which was not available before. The perpetrators of these reductions of religion

6

were neither idiots nor frauds and none of their theories is wholly devoid of truth. This being so, and it being the task of the Christian apologist to seek truth wherever it is to be found, there is an obligation incumbent on him, or rather an opportunity open to him to deepen or enrich his understanding of religion or faith by acknowledging and appropriating the element of truth that is there. One only has to look back to the controversies that raged all over the Western world in the nineteenth century over the question of evolution, Darwin's *Origin of Species* and all that. To those who held the orthodox belief that the Bible was the inspired Word of God, and who interpreted this to mean that every word must be literally true in a historical or scientific sense, the claim that the human race had evolved naturally from other species of animal life obviously sounded like a flat contradiction of their belief. Did not the book of Genesis make it quite clear that the whole world of nature, including man, had been made by God's fiat in six days, and moreover that all humanity were not only descended from one couple, Adam and Eve, but were radically affected by their sin? Clearly, if the Bible was right, Darwin was wrong, and if Darwin was right, the Bible must be wrong – but that could not be. So Darwin's claim must be wrong and be shown to be wrong.

It took many decades, even generations, of agonising, sometimes bitter controversy, with many wreckages on the way, for the situation to be clarified, so that now most Christians[4] have no difficulty in allowing truth to both Darwin and to the early chapters of Genesis. For now, they are able to understand the creation stories in Genesis not as quasi-scientific or historical accounts of 'how-it-all-began', but much more as a picture in highly coloured, dramatic and therefore memorable terms of how things stand between God the Creator and his creation (including his human creatures) now. Understood in this way, the Genesis stories can have an immediacy, an impact, a relevance to their modern readers and to modern believers far more pointed than in the calmer days prior to the controversy over Darwinism. From this point of view, it can be claimed now with some justice that that controversy, far from threatening the faith, in the long term actually assisted believers to come to a deeper and more pertinent understanding of certain key biblical passages.

This study is undertaken in the hope that it will be possible, by

7

considering various attempts to explain away religious faith, to unearth positive contributions to a deeper, fuller understanding. In this sense, while it will involve a certain amount of defensive work in outlining some of the arguments that can be made against attacks, the underlying emphasis will be on attempting, as one who stands within the faith, to use these attacks on the faith as the occasion and the means of understanding the faith better. In other words, its aim is constructive rather than merely defensive.

In these days when we are conscious of the difficulties of communication between separated groups, the young and the old, the classes, the nations of the West and the nations of the Third World, in these days of apparent lack of communication it is cause for real encouragement that when open discussion between disagreeing parties really does take place, then it can be followed by growth in understanding. This happens within Christianity, for example, when Protestants and Catholics really speak to each other in a spirit uncrushed by defensiveness, and try to explain, in language which the other can understand, what they really mean by certain notions which seem to divide – like 'infallibility' for Catholics or 'the authority of the Bible' for Protestants. The very attempt to put what one believes into someone else's language offers new insight into the belief.

This also happens across religious boundaries. One of the features of European society during the last quarter century has been the springing up of groups engaged in dialogue of one kind or another. One such group in which I was personally involved was a group of twelve, six Christians and six Marxists who met regularly to discuss matters of mutual interest. One winter evening, I went along to the meeting to discover that although the six Marxists were there, 'flu had smitten the five other Christians, including the one who was to lead the discussion that night. After various illegitimate suggestions had been offered as to why Christians were so prone to disease, it was suggested that I as a Christian should try to explain to the Marxists what I meant by 'faith'. This I attempted to do and a lively discussion followed as I was quizzed on what I had said. I do not know how much the Marxists actually learned that night. I do know, however, that the attempt to express what I understood by 'faith' in a way that had any chance at all of being understood by these people with their alien presuppositions taught me a great deal: it enabled me to see things in a new way, and far from being destructive of what I believed proved considerably fortifying.

Defence of the faith which is not open to new insights or light or colour stands little chance of helping anyone, in understanding or in faith. It is to be hoped that this will not be forgotten as we proceed to examine the first of my reductionists or 'explainers away'.

I

SIGMUND FREUD

1856–1939

A Psychological Explanation

Freud's explanation of religion was by no means the first human attempt to explain religion away. The ancient Greeks, to go no farther back than that, knew all about it. Yet it is sensible to begin with Freud because it is his work and reputation, and, rather more to the point, potted versions of his theory that have more than any other left their mark on the Western mid-twentieth-century mind. It would be foolish not to acknowledge that he is still looked upon, not to say revered, by all sorts and conditions as one of the great liberators of mankind – and womankind, of course, – particularly in the realm of the sexual. In fact, and by any standard, Sigmund Freud is one of the giants who stand at the gate of the twentieth century, a daring thinker, a pioneer in psychology, and, perhaps above all, a truly courageous man. One would have to be peculiarly insensitive, even bigoted, not to be moved by his life's story.[1]

Jewish by birth and upbringing, though not by religious faith he was followed most of his days by anti-Semitism, crude, strident and bitter, eventually, with the advent of Hitler, driving him, a refugee, to England in the last years of his life from the Vienna where he had made his reputation and spent all but his first three years. In his early days, it retarded the progress and promotion a student and researcher of his brilliance might otherwise have expected. It gave those who felt threatened by his theories and the novelty of his practice a handy weapon with which to ridicule them, and deny them a fair hearing. It is by no means surprising that for him the term 'Christian' carried association far beyond the religious.

It is mildly ironic that for all his reputation as a liberator in matters of sex, his biographer, Ernest Jones (also his colleague and friend), can describe him as 'monogamic and uxorious',[2] which presumably means that he was a 'one-woman man' and a good family man. During the five years of his engagement, necessitated by the need to accumulate enough money to set up house, he wrote his fiancée some nine hundred letters. With his six children, there is no doubt that he was a loving father, though perhaps an indulgent one. Some of his views would certainly be condemned as sexist today. For example, discussing the views of J. S. Mill (whose works he translated into German) on the equality of women, Freud concluded:

> I believe that all reforming action in law and education would break down in front of the fact that, long before the age at which man can earn a position in society, Nature has determined woman's destiny through beauty, charm, and sweetness. Law and custom have much to given women that has been withheld from them, but the position of women will surely be what it is: in youth an adored darling and in mature years a loved wife.[3]

Freud trained as a doctor in Vienna, and after passing his final medical examinations spent several years practising in hospital there. His early specialization was in neuro-pathology, in which he was appointed a lecturer, and in the course of his researches in this connection he made some important discoveries about the drug cocaine. Much more important, however, became his interest in neuroses, their causes and treatment, the investigation of the unconscious through psycho-analysis, in short, psycho-pathology, and it is in this field that he established his reputation. His first major work, *The Interpretation of Dreams*[4] was published in the last months of 1899 (the publisher taking the liberty of printing 1900 on the book!) and although it was ten years before it began to make an impact and twenty before its impact reverberated internationally, it is still considered a classic. Ernest Jones wrote of it thus:

> It is Freud's most original work. The main conclusions in it were entirely novel and unexpected. This applies to the theme proper, that of dream structure and to the many themes that appear incidentally. The most important of the latter is the description of the now familiar 'Oedipus complex' – the erotic and the hostile relations of child to parent are frankly exposed. Together with this goes the appreciation of infantile life and its overwhelming im-

portance for all the innumerable developments that make up the adult human body. Above all, not only does it afford a secure basis for the theory of the unconscious in man but also provides one of the best modes of approach to this dark region, so much more important in man's actual behaviour than his consciousness. Freud very justly termed the interpretation of dreams the *via regia* to the unconscious. The book, moreover, contains a host of suggestions in the fields of literature, mythology and education – the famous footnote on Hamlet is a striking example – which have since provided the inspiration for a great number of special studies.[5]

Teacher, researcher, author, throughout he practised as a therapist, deriving an enormous bank of data from the dreams, experiences, fears, frustrations and above all neuroses of his patients, data on which he drew with immense skill in his psychological theories, and later, his wider speculations.

His reputation gradually spread, with the result not only that patients came to him from all over the world, but in many places abroad, his principles and practice found followers who were themselves prepared to learn and practise. Not only followers, however, appeared, but ostracism by much of the medical establishment at home meant that it was virtually inevitable that sharp resistance should be found abroad. As early as 1908, a Presbyterian minister in Australia, Dr Donald Fraser, had to leave the ministry because of his sympathy with Freud's work. At the First International Congress of Psychiatry and Neurology, at Amsterdam in 1907, a famous German neurologist[6] promised that no patient of his should ever be allowed to reach any of Freud's followers, with their 'conscienceless descent into absolute filth (*Schweinerei*)'.

Despite the fact that his theories flourished and an army of Freudian practitioners appeared throughout the Western world, all along there was opposition, controversy and prejudice. In his declining years, far from easing, things got worse. Physically, Freud had to endure for years an extremely painful cancer of the mouth. Gradually, with the rise of Hitler and the Nazis, prejudice grew into persecution of him as a Jew, he saw his work in Germany and in Austria totally impeded, and eventually, though he left it until the last possible moment, he was forced to leave his home in Vienna and take refuge for the last few years of his life, an exile, in England.

However moved we may be by his life story, and however impressed by his technical achievements as a pioneer psychologist and psychotherapist, we must now try to give an account of his views on religion. He was not a religious man himself. Although he was not ashamed of his Jewish background – indeed he was ashamed of his father, who on one occasion told him of an incident in which he had accepted, passively, crude anti-Semitic prejudice in action – he was in no sense a religious man. For himself, he saw no need for it, derived no benefit from it, simply assuming that it responded to nothing 'real' in the world, or – but for him this would be an irrational concept – beyond it. Indeed, during his lengthy engagement, one of his chief worries was lest he be forced to go through the traditional Jewish marriage ceremony.[7] If he was not interested in or needful of religion for himself, he was nonetheless intensely interested in why other people should need it, why, in the history of mankind, it should have played such a predominant role. Why should it have been necessary? What caused men and women, through the centuries, apparently from the earliest times, to believe? He discovered clues towards answering these questions from the evidence provided in his consulting room by the patients who came to him for help.

One of his contributions to psychology was to produce evidence of 'the infant that lives on in the grown man'. Each stage of infancy and early childhood gives rise to certain tensions, and if these tensions are not satisfactorily resolved, they are, as it were, driven underground, below the level of consciousness, into the unconscious. There they are not necessarily buried, but may manifest themselves in later life in irrational, unusual, 'neurotic' symptoms, behaviour which seems unnecessary to the onlooker but which is apparently very necessary for the well-being of the subject. Freud's theory was that if the roots of these neurotic symptoms could be unearthed, if the unresolved tensions of which they were the expression could be brought from the darkness of the unconscious to the daylight of consciousness, then the patient would be able to acknowledge them and accept them, and he would be cured. The method which Freud developed for facilitating this process of unearthing and bringing to the surface what might lie deep in the unconscious was psycho-analysis.

Now the more Freud discovered about neurosis, the more he was struck by the resemblance between the behaviour of his neurotic patients and what he believed to be the behaviour of religious people. For him, observing religion very much from the outside, and taking the kind of Roman Catholicism practised in the Austria of his day very much as the model of all religious practice, he understood it largely as a matter of the believer performing certain specific practices, observances, ceremonials and rites. Thus regarding it, he was struck how much there seemed to be in common between religious practice and the behaviour he had come to recognize in his consulting room as neurotic. The neurotic signs he identified in his patients – the private ceremonials obsessively indulged in, like persistent hand-washing rituals, irrational tidying routines, – rituals which had a meaning for the unconscious apart from which they would have been incomprehensible, these seemed to Freud to be paralleled by the meticulous observance of religious rites and ceremonials by the religious person, indeed too closely paralleled to be accounted for as mere coincidence.

Following up this line of reasoning, Freud was able to point to other similarities between the neurotic and the religious person. He noted the common phenomenon of troubled conscience which followed any omission of the neurotic's ceremonial or the religious person's rite. Both groups treated their subject of ceremonial as isolated from everything else in life, and therefore on no account to be disturbed. Both seemed to share an underlying sense of guilt, against which the ceremonials or rites are observed as a defence – against punishment. In both sets of circumstance, renunciation of instinct was involved, in the case of the neurotic, usually the sexual instinct, in the case of the religious person usually the egoistic or anti-social instinct. In each group, something like acts of penance were necessary, of considerable importance for the peace of mind of the subject. Finally, he observed in each case what he called the 'mechanism of psychical displacement', by which he meant a psychical value being given to the ceremonial or rite out of all proportion to its intrinsic importance. Freud did concede that there were certain differences to be discerned between the religious' and the neurotic's behaviour, but for him these were not differences of quality. The similarities were too close, and constrained him to the verdict that religion was best understood as a neurosis, and in view of its place in the history of mankind, a universal neurosis, a 'universal obsessional neurosis'.

Like all neuroses, it ought to be treated as a sickness, and if this were done it could be 'cured' like all neuroses, by analytical methods. When the religious practitioner understood why he was indulging in such neurotic behaviour, he would be enabled to accept the 'real' situation and face reality without resort to the defence of religion.

Freud's interest in religion was by no means exhausted by this conclusion. What was it, he wanted to know, that was responsible for the origin and persistence of this universal obsessional neurosis that is religion? Having found the clue to much abnormal adult behaviour in the experiences and tensions of infancy or early childhood, he was drawn to seek the answer in the childhood of the human race, in primitive society. His anthropological researches [8] when set alongside his investigations into the human psyche led him to the exciting conclusion that 'the beginnings of religion . . . meet in the Oedipus complex'. [9] Freud believed that all races had passed through a stage of totemism, a system in which the beginnings of social and religious practice are to be observed. In this stage, the whole of life is dominated by a few 'taboo' prohibitions.

The totem was usually an animal of some kind, which stood in a peculiarly close relation to the tribe, and the main prohibitions were two in number: the prohibition or taboo against killing the totem animal, and the prohibition or taboo against males having sexual relations with any women of the same clan, that is, against incest. Now when Freud compared these two principal taboos with the main elements of the ancient myth of King Oedipus, who killed his father and took his mother as wife, the similarities were too good to miss. Obviously, the totem must be a substitute for a physical father, and the conclusion Freud was driven to was that here was the starting point of the formation of religion – totemism, the nucleus of which is the killing of the father. This tied in well with Freud's claim, allegedly based on observation, that in every case there was a direct relationship between a person's image or picture of God and his image or picture of his physical father.

15

In his anthropological researches, Freud also came across the phenomenon of the 'totem feast'. This occurred usually once a year: the totem animal was ritually slaughtered, devoured and mourned over. This ritual meal seemed to give the clan communion with the totem or father-figure, and with that the protection which was needed. More than that, it provided a very suggestive parallel with later eucharistic or communion meals.

In his speculations concerning the beginnings of religion, Freud went even further. He tidied up his conjectures with his vision or hypothesis of the 'primal horde'. This went somewhat as follows: the sole ruler of the clan was the father, who had exclusive rights over the women of the clan and who drove the sons away as potential rivals. The sons admired the father for his power, but also resented it, so one day they came together and united to overwhelm the father, killing and devouring him who had been their enemy, but also their ideal. The deed being done, the sons quarrelled, but eventually came to an agreement and formed a clan in which the practice of totemism had a decisive role. Its role was to prevent the repetition of such a deed, and to prevent the possession of women of the same clan, for whom they had killed their father. The totem feast was a commemoration or re-enactment of that primal murder. In Freud's own words:

> After they (the sons) had satisfied their hate by his removal, and had carried out their wish for identification with him, the suppressed tender impulses had to assert themselves. This took the form of remorse, a sense of guilt was formed which coincided here with the remorse generally felt. The dead now became stronger than the living had been, even as we observe it to-day in the destinies of men. . . . They undid their deed by declaring that the killing of the father substitute, the totem, was not allowed, and renounced the fruits of their deed by denying themselves the liberated women. Thus they created the two fundamental taboos of totemism out of the sense of guilt of the sons, and for this very reason had to correspond with the two repressed wishes of the Oedipus Complex. Whoever disobeyed became guilty of the only two crimes which troubled primitive society.[10]

After a while, the totem no longer acted as an effective substitute for the father, who became the proto-type of God himself. No one knows how this happened, but psycho-analytical investigation indicates that God is in every case modelled after the father and that our personal relation to God is dependant on our relation to our physical father, changing and fluctuating with him. At bottom, God is nothing but an exalted father.

The sense of guilt deriving from this primal crime has affected all mankind, and various religions are various attempts to deal with it. Christianity's case is obvious. In Freud's interpretation, Christ is to be understood as having taken his own life to expiate for his brothers' primal crime. At the same time, however, he took revenge on the father on his brothers' behalf, and this he did by becoming, as son, a god in place of the father.

Having then diagnosed religion as a 'universal obsessional neurosis' and having, by his way of it, successfully accounted for its origins, he was in a position to sum it all up, and this he did – as an illusion. In his late work, *The Future of an Illusion* (1927)[11], the illusion is religion – and it has no future. Like culture, religion is explained as man's defence against the forces of nature, 'sublime, pitiless, inexorable'. Just as the infant, helpless and terrified, needs protection from natural forces which threaten him and finds it in the love of the parent, particularly the father, so the adult, beset with the feelings of helplessness, also needs protection and finds it by continuing to believe in the existence of an all-powerful father, benevolently ruling, establishing a moral order, overcoming the sharpness of death. What is happening here is the classic case of the well-known psychological mechanism of projection – the adult externalizes or projects outside him so as to make it an external reality a defence against an inner conflict or need. This has been maintained generation after generation not by reason, but by rationalization, with every possible kind of insincerity and intellectual misdemeanour. Moreover, such is the sanctity of religious dogmas and propositions that it is forbidden to raise the question of their authenticity at all.

Religion, then, is an illusion, wish-fulfilment, a protection against reality. Through the ages, men and women have thought that in their worship, their prayers and their theology they were responding to a reality other than themselves, but they were wrong. All they were doing – though they were unaware of it and though they had, as a necessary defence against the blind and merciless forces of nature, good motives for doing it – was projecting and rationalizing. Now, however, that people recognize what has been going on, projecting, rationalizing, and know or can know the nature of the universe in which they live and of which they form part (it being taken for granted that 'this-is-all-there-is', that which can be seen, touched, heard, smelt or spoken exhausts the whole of reality), now that people have, if they would only but recognize it, in psychoanalysis the tool which enables them to be revealed to themselves as they really are, they will soon be equipped to face the cruel facts of nature, reality, without having to resort to the fraudulent aid of religion.

Freud is not sanguine about the eventual outcome. His is no easy forecast of a future of sweetness and light for humanity. Religion in the past has fulfilled a genuine role in offering protection from the alien forces which encumber mankind. A future without religion is by no means secure. But there can be no going back. Present and future generations must have the courage to face the truth, and as they do this the illusion that is religion will have come to an end.

Here, then, is an interpretation of religion which offers to explain how it arose, to show what is actually going on when people believe in God or worship him or talk about him, and to point the way forward to mankind to stand on its own feet, to accept the brute facts of nature and reality and to dispense with the illusion which is religion and which has hitherto seemed necessary for survival. Moreover, it is an interpretation which seems on the face of it to have scientific backing, being allegedly based on observation – of infant behaviour, of adult patients' actions and reactions, and on the beliefs and practices of primitive tribes. Moreover, it is not difficult to follow or understand. It is not surprising, therefore, that it should seem so plausible, nor that it should have commended itself to a wide, popular audience, looking for 'scientific explanations', in an age when only science seemed able to provide reliable answers. There are many points in Freud's explanation which do indeed appeal to common sense, and, more than that, which have proved to be of invaluable help to pastors, theologians and believers, seeking to understand and work out their faith consistently. Some indication of these constructive points will be given before this chapter is ended.

First, however, it is necessary to offer some sort of comment on what is, after all, a serious attempt, under the guise of science, to dispose of religion as anything other than an illusion.

Perhaps the first thing that should arouse caution against accepting Freud's account of religion uncritically is the fact that so many of Freud's claims and conclusions are no longer accepted without a great deal of qualification by those in his own fields of psychology and psychiatry. His claims to scientific objectivity have been widely rejected, the validity of his procedures queried, and the virtual unfalsifiability of many of his conclusions pointed to. Doubtless some of the prejudice which he experienced during his life-time still persists, but the fact is that he is not entitled to be sheltered from the criticisms of those who disagree with him under the umbrella of science. His speculations about a primal horde, for example, as indeed much of what he accepted as 'fact' about totem and taboo, seem now to be without much scientific basis.[12] This is not to say that he was either a charlatan or a fool – his achievements in helping suffering men and women make such charges, even though levelled at him during his life, outrageous. Neither is it to say that his conclusions about religion on these grounds alone were necessarily wrong. It simply means that they were not necessarily right and deserve no additional respect or attention for being 'scientific'. This seems now to be widely admitted, even by those who recognize Frued's originality and who would claim him as one of the great prophets of the early twentieth century.

An illustration of the unprovability, or rather unfalsifiability, of Freud's claims is his contention that religion is a 'universal obsessional neurosis', originating in some unresolved conflict of infancy or early childhood. How is this to be tested? What evidence would Freud accept for an exception to this rule? It is hard to envisage any. It is also hard to see how Freud would protect himself from a tables-turning exercise on himself, in terms of which it might be maintained that if religious belief is the consequence of an unresolved conflict, so rejection of religious belief might be no less a consequence of infantile conflict, rationalized into an intellectual system. *NB* What is sauce for the goose is sauce for the gander – in logic, if not in charity – and it has, in fact, often been pointed out that Freud's earliest acquaintance with religion was being taken by his Roman

Catholic nanny to mass when he was a toddler. But this same nanny was, when he was still very young, dismissed by his parents – for theft – and it does not take too much imagination to envisage the possible alien associations which this traumatic event would stir up in the infant Freudian mind!

There is no need, however, to lay all the blame at the door of the wretched Christian nanny. One can argue quite logically that if religion is at bottom only an extension of a man's attitude to his physical father, then hatred and resentment of one's physical father must issue in rejection of religion, or atheism. This is, in other words, a circular argument. The story is told of a famous archbishop, addressing a student audience in the thirties when Freudian theory was all the undergraduate rage. A superior student suggested to the archbishop: 'You only believe what you believe because of your early upbringing.' To which the reply came back in a flash: 'And you only believe that I only believe what I believe because of my early upbringing because of your early upbringing.' [13] The argument is indeed circular. This does not again prove that Freud was wrong: it merely shows that he was not necessarily right.

There is another logical point that needs to be made in this connection. This is that to make a claim about the cause or psychological origin of a belief is not to say anything about its truth or falsehood. To pretend otherwise is to be guilty of what is known in logic as the 'genetic fallacy'. Freud thought he had discovered why people believe in God, he thought he could point to the origin of or cause of their believing, and concluded from this that such belief must be illusory. But that is an entirely illegitimate conclusion. Everyone accepts that $8 \times 8 = 64$. The psychological origin or cause of their accepting this is almost certainly not that they have worked out and understood a rather complicated mathematical system: much more likely that they feared the wrath of the teacher, if not the rap across the knuckles, if they got the answer wrong when asked to recite it. But it is still true that $8 \times 8 = 64$, even if the motive of any given individual for accepting it as true is no worthier than fear of punishment or hope of reward. H. H. Farmer recalled that he once had an argument with a man, lost his temper and called him 'a bumptious ass'. To this the man replied: 'You couldn't be so rude unless you were jealous.' At this point a third party intervened: 'You

20

are both right. You [to the one] spoke out of jealousy' And you [to the other] have been a bumptious ass.'[14] In other words, motive, however worthy or unworthy, does not affect the truth or falsehood of what is said.

Again, this does not prove that Freud was necessarily wrong in his conjectures about religion. What it does suggest, however, is that psychological data and psychological conclusions cannot and need not now claim to show that religious assertions are in themselves illusory, unreasonable or, in face of all the evidence, false. As a matter of fact, Freud himself came rather close to admitting this in *The Future of an Illusion*.[15] Yet this did not curb him in his speculations as to the origins and nature of religion. The truth is that Freud was a convinced atheist long before he began his psychological researches. Long before he met a neurotic patient, he had decided that religious beliefs were irrational, and needed both to be explained and explained away.

Perhaps this explains why he missed a further point which seems rather obvious. If religion is best understood as a neurosis, why do the fruits of religion not resemble more closely the kind of behaviour normally associated with neurosis? Would one not expect the most serious or intense practitioners of religion to share to the highest degree the fate and exhibit to a marked degree the signs of those who indulge in prolonged fantasy thinking, i.e., not only external disaster but arrest of growth and disintegration of personality? Is this in fact what one finds? It is impossible to claim perfect objectivity here, and certainly it would not be difficult, in surveying the calendar of Christian saints, to find some whose behaviour, for all its sanctity, was distinctly odd to say the least. Nevertheless, it is perhaps fair comment to suggest that the models of the religious life whom most contemporary Christians admire and emulate are not those who display what William James once called a 'crippled holiness'. They are rather those who seem to embody the qualities of selflessness, growth towards wholeness, 'moral helpfulness'.[16] If these are the consequence of the neurosis which, according to Freud, is religion, then they are consequences which are not found following any other kind of neurosis. If religious experience does issue in the service of mankind, as well as the alleged service of God – and very few Christian people nowadays would recognize it as service of God if it did not also issue in service of mankind – then if this is an illusion it is a unique illusion for which even psycho-analysis could be no substitute. Of course, this kind of reasoning involves a value judgment as to the reality of a person's life: in simple terms, that kindness is better than cruelty, that it is better to help than to exploit. But this is a value judgment which psychology, with its insights into motivation and personality, far from restraining, encourages us to make.[17]

In the last resort, the point which strikes Christian believers most forcibly as they attempt to understand Freud's explanations of religion is the dissimilarity between the God whom Freud describes as being believed in and the God whom Christians themselves try to worship and serve. For Freud, God is not only always modelled on the human father, his principal function seems to be to offer protection from punishment as well as from the harsh, pitiless and inexorable forces of nature, in return for loyalty and obedience: a supernatural benevolent despot. Doubtless this is how Christian talk about God and worship of him appeared to Freud from the outside. There is no suggestion of fraudulent misrepresentation on Freud's part. Yet it is hardly surprising if Christians, from the 'inside' of faith, as it were, find it impossible to recognize their God in the one whom Freud describes. It is perfectly true that Christians describe their God as a Father, and a 'loving, heavenly Father', at that. It is also true that if there were absolutely no similarity or points of contact between what has been understood as a human father and what has been believed about God, then God would not have been referred to as Father in the first place, and would not so be referred to now. Yet this does not mean that what Christians have in mind when they think of God as Father is primarily his power and willingness to guarantee those who do obeisance to him protection from external disaster and immunity from the effects of guilt or from extinction. In calling God 'Father', they are trying to indicate and express a much more dynamic relationship between themselves and God, a relationship more accurately reflected in terms of 'love' (a reciprocal relationship) rather than protective power. What defines their understanding of the Fatherhood of God is finally not guesswork, speculation or wishful thinking. Rather it is centred, or summed up in what they believe concerning Jesus of Nazareth. In his life, and supremely in his death, Christians see God disclosing himself at his deepest and most personal in an identification which is total. Yet here, supremely, is no retreat into supernatural security, no flight into infancy, no refuge in illusion, religious or otherwise. Here is a man living a life of love in action, who in lonely realism 'set his face stedfastly to Jerusalem', to a future which was anything but secure. Moreover, he offered his disciples no *quid pro quo* in exchange for their allegiance – the theological point behind the important doctrine of 'justification by grace' – rather the Christian church has at its best always understood his invitation to disciples to be:

> if any man would come after me, let him deny himself and take up his cross and follow me (Matt. 16.24 RSV).

If this is the authentic emphasis, as Christians at least understand it to be, then it is impossible to see how it can accurately be interpreted by the Freudian scheme.

There seem then to be abundant and valid reasons for returning a confident verdict of 'not proven' to Freud's claim to have explained religion in general and Christianity in particular in terms of illusion, to be accounted for by reference to psychological origins. The evidence he offers simply does not justify the claim. There is, indeed, no need to use a sledgehammer to drive this home. Most psychologists – even those who work most closely with Freudian categories – have for long admitted this and would have no difficulty in agreeing with the judgment of the author of an introduction to psychology of religion, written some forty years ago:

> The truth of the primary assumption of the real existence of that all-inclusive and supreme Other to which we give the name of God is a matter not for the psychologist but for the metaphysician, or perhaps for the saint. The psychologist can do no more than examine our response to the ultimate reality, so far as that course can be seen and recorded. Our beliefs and worship, and for that matter our sins lie open to his inspection. God does not.[18]

Once this point is accepted, the believer can cease to be defensive about Freud's insights into religion. In fact, he must do so, unless he wishes to dispense with glimpses of truth that may turn out to be of

23

the greatest importance in helping him to understand his faith better. It is to this positive, constructive task that we now turn.

Consider, for example, Freud's contention that God is in every case modelled after the father and that our personal relation to God is dependant upon our relation to our physical father, fluctuating with him and that God is at bottom nothing but an exalted father, arrived at by a process of projection. This contention ought, on valid grounds, to be rejected as a complete statement of the case of belief in God, and it certainly does not justify the conclusion which Freud drew that religion is therefore illusory. But it does not follow that there is therefore no truth whatever in it.

God an exalted father, a father-substitute, a wish-fulfiller? No believer would admit this, but there must be very few sensitive observers, pastors for example, who have not known people whose God is just that, or seems to be. For some believers, their God seems to exist for no better reason than to offer them protection and guarantee them and theirs a rosy future, without much regard for anyone else. Such a God has always been recognizable as a false God, in the Judaeo-Christian tradition inveighed against with unrelenting prophetic pressure and irony throughout the centuries. It is Freud's great achievement to have offered categories to enable us to understand psychologically when people are tying themselves to these false gods. They are an illusion. But faith's task, in the face of their exposure, is not to abandon all belief in God, but rather to make room for him who comes from beyond and is not under our unconscious control. An eminent French philosopher puts it this way: 'Biblical faith represents God – the God of the prophets and the God of Christian Trinity – as a Father. Atheism [he here refers to the philosopher Nietzsche as well as Freud] teaches us to renounce this father image. Overcome as an idol, the father may be recovered as a symbol, however. . . . An idol must die, in order that a symbol of Being may speak.'[19] If Freud performs this service for believers, it is service of the highest order.

The idea of 'projection', too, is one which deserves close scrutiny by those who want to take religion seriously. Freud concluded that if there was any element of projection present the resultant belief must be illusory. This simply does not follow. There are false projections, assuredly, leading to illusory conclusions, but that is certainly not an exhaustive description of the situation. There are projections which

24

are not necessarily false, which may, on the contrary, be the only route towards an understanding of the truth. When faced with the unknown, if we are to talk about it at all, the only language available to us is the language of our own experience, which means that an element of projection is inevitable. Freud's own interpretation of reality was in strictly materialistic terms, excluding any possible reference to anything or 'matter' not observable and describable in objective scientific terms. Yet this view of reality undoubtedly contains an element of projection from his own experience, but was, for Freud, not thereby invalidated.

Similarly, it is not in the least unreasonable for the believer to admit that there is an element of projection in his talk about God. This of itself is not fatal to belief. What must necessarily follow if it is not to become fatal to belief is an openness to testing, probing, comparing by reference to experience in order to judge whether what was initially a projection 'fits' or not. Attention has sometimes been drawn to the similarity between projection and the application of a hypothesis in scientific enquiry. A hypothesis is formed and then tested where relevant, in an attempt to show conclusively through some sort of sifting process that it is not false. Similarly with the process of projection. The believer must be prepared to qualify the projection if it does not fit.

Thus, to return to Freud's key example, when believers first refer to God as 'Father', they can probably only initially understand this as a projection of their own experience of their father (which, incidentally, makes it such a difficult concept for those who never knew their father or who would rather forget him, to apply to God). But there is no other starting point than the human one. When, however, the concept Father is applied to God, because of the other things that require to be said about God, the concept acquires additional associations, becomes refined and redefined. When that happens, this redefined sense becomes the paradigm or key to all understanding of fatherhood, feeding back, as it were, and giving a new perspective on what could be meant by human fatherhood. Without something like the mechanism of 'projection', this could never have happened – and acknowledgment is due to Freud for enabling us to see this. But Freud's formula – that in the realm of religion, 'projection' equals 'false projection' – cannot reasonably be supported.

Something may be said of the process of 'rationalization', to which

25

Freud was so sensitive and which in his view so markedly character-ized religious belief. Much of human reasoning is largely determined by what is wished or desired, and it is immense gain to have psy-chological tools to describe and identify what is going on. As we have seen, Freud claimed that all religious doctrine was to be ex-plained in terms of rationalization and was thereby shown to be false. We have sufficiently indicated why this does not follow, or if it does, that it must affect all psychological teaching as well as religi-ous. It could, of course be added here, that Freud rather seriously overlooked the sensitivity to this process which is evident in religious traditions themselves: the practice of self-examination and confess-ion; the prophetic warnings against, for example, the human heart, 'deceitful above all things and desperately wicked: who can know it?' (Jer. 17.9). What now needs to be acknowledged is that when we have got over and resisted Freud's alleged disposal of religion, his understanding of the process of rationalization can be of the greatest possible help in the living as well as the understanding of the life of faith.

Most obviously, it is in the realm of pastoral help and counselling that this is evident. It apparently came as something of a surprise to Freud himself to discover this. One of the most unlikely friendships of all time was formed between Freud and the Swiss Calvinist pastor Oskar Pfister, who was interested not so much in Freud's explana-tion of religion as in the application of Freudian techniques and analyses towards relieving psychological disorders receiving religious expression and distorting the religious life. In 1909, Freud wrote to Pfister:

> In itself, psycho-analysis is neither religious nor the opposite, but an impartial instrument which can serve the clergy as well as the laity when it is used only to free suffering people. I have been very struck at realising how I had never thought of the extra-ordinary help the psycho-analytic method can be in pastoral work, probably because wicked heretics like us are so far away from that circle.[20]

Whether Freud himself realized it or not, his account of the dyna-mics of human personality have proved of the greatest possible value to pastors in helping those who have sought their counsel to work their way through a crippling, self-enclosing, bogus or illusory religion of self-preservation and fear to an open and healthy relationship with God and their fellows. Without insights originally deriving from Freud, it would have been impossible for a writer like H. A. Williams, for example, to expose so expertly the 'artful dodges' which can often be practised and the pious guises which can often be adopted in the name of religion to avoid acceptance of oneself as one really is, to enable one to pretend one is serving God when one is really only serving oneself, to satisfy unacknowledged needs, to conceal inflated guilt feelings, to provide an illusory religious shield which offers protection as much from the real God as from the real world.[21]

Freud is not, of course, the sole parent of modern pastoral counselling but it would be impossible to consider Freud and religion without paying tribute to his positive, though possibly unwitting, contribution. This having been insisted upon, however, it is equally necessary to insist that when he went beyond the workings of the human psyche in its response to reality to a dogmatic assertion of what this reality could or could not be, thereby excluding the reality of God and of appropriate response to him, he wandered into fields of speculation far removed from what was justified either by logic or by his observations.

The Freudian reduction of religion has undoubtedly had a good innings. For generations of the twenties, thirties, forties and fifties of this century, and perhaps some of the sixties and seventies, he has seemed to provide a scientific basis for disbelief in God, for writing him off as an illusion born of wishful thinking and intimately connected with the Oedipus complex. It must be clear that this innings is now over. Too many people who have taken the trouble to examine his claims regarding religion and the evidence on which they are allegedly based have found them, on the basis of the evidence, unjustified, if not altogether plain false. It would, however, be a bad case of over-reaction if such findings were used as an excuse not to listen to Freud at all. He has still insight to offer to the working of the human mind and the development of the human personality. The man or woman of faith has a mind, is a personality like any other, and if he or she would understand the mind and personality, and the behaviour that accompanies it, Freud and his successors in the field of psychology still have rich resources to offer – without prejudice – from their store.

2

KARL MARX

1818–1883

The Marxist Explanation

In turning from Sigmund Freud to Karl Marx, we are, as it were, turning from a minor prophet to a major one. Although educated people in the West are probably more familiar with some of the details of Freud's thinking than of Marx's, this certainly would not be true in a global context. The fact is that something like one third of the world's inhabitants live in societies whose official aims and outlooks and ways of looking at the world are highly coloured if not totally conditioned by Marxist thinking. For them, Freud's theories are written off as the typical intellectual product of a Western bourgeois reactionary, and on this account robbed of credibility. For them, assessments of religion and attitudes to religion, 'what everybody knows' about religion, is what is derived from official Communist teaching, and official Communist teaching is, of course, everywhere, heavily indebted to the thinking of Karl Marx. If, therefore, one is in the least interested in what a very large minority of the world's population thinks of religion, then there can be no alternative to going to the source of what is now considered natural and taken for granted and trying to unearth Karl Marx's own judgment.

Marx himself was at one time a Christian. He was born in 1818 and brought up in what was then Rhenish Prussia. His antecedents were Jewish, but his father, a lawyer, became a Christian and the whole family was baptised. There is some evidence to the effect that Marx's father owed his conversion not so much to any cataclysmic religious experience as to a (perfectly natural) desire to get on in his profession in a country officially Christian and where discrimination against Jews in all sorts of ways was not only a thing of the future.

28

However that may be, Marx was certainly not brought up in an atmosphere of heavy piety: 'free thinking' was probably the order of the day.

It would be an exaggeration to say that Marx had absolutely no interest in religion at any time. While he was at school, he wrote an essay on St John's Gospel, which was highly commended. It has even been suggested that as an adolescent he was a serious, even passionate Christian.[1] Whether this is true or not, the fact is that an atmosphere of liberalism and rationalism, with widespread tolerance, pervaded his home when he was young, and by the years of maturity he had repudiated any personal interest in things religious, an interest which never returned. There is no evidence that he himself ever experienced or even ever appreciated the emotional depths of religion, and although he did pass through a phase of extremely cerebral 'Christianity', while he was a student in Berlin (one scholar actually dates this 'during or immediately after 1837')[2] he became philosophically a naturalist, a realist, a materialist and an atheist. From such a stance, he never subsequently moved.

For one who during his life wrote a great deal, and who could say that 'the criticism of religion is the beginning of all criticism'[3], it is perhaps surprising that he did not have more to say specifically on the nature of religion in general and Christianity in particular. He was after all, brought up and worked, until he was banned, in an overtly 'Christian' state, Prussia. Part of the reason for this is undoubtedly that the major task of criticizing religion was already being done, and, in his view, successfully being done by others, and although they did not go far enough for him, it was not necessary for him to work over again with his spade the same soil as other philosophers of religion had done. Most influential among these 'spade-workers' were the philosophers Friedrich Hegel (1770–1831) and Ludwig Feuerbach (1804–1872), and it is impossible to understand Marx's views on religion out of relation to those of Hegel, and above all, Feuerbach.

There is a lively debate in progress as to the extent to which Marx was a Hegelian. It is not necessary to enter it here, save to say that on the one hand, he was influenced by many of Hegel's individual ideas and developed them: history as the place where something was going on, something which led to freedom; the dialectical method as the appropriate one to understand something that is not static but on the move; the concept of alienation or 'self-estrangement' whereby people, work and human institutions become objectified, and man becomes a stranger in the world that he has made: all these, and many other elements were taken over by Marx and used by him for his own purposes and in his own way. This is perhaps not surprising, given Hegel's extraordinary influence in Germany, and not only in Germany. Marx himself testified that wherever he went in philosophy, all roads ended with Hegel. On the other hand, it is equally clear that he rejected without compromise Hegel's system as a whole. More than that, he could refer to him with contempt as a 'sophist', 'throwing trivialities around', offering 'inconsistencies and drunken speculations'. There is, fortunately, no need here to attempt a judgment on Hegel's influence on Marx, save to say that certain Hegelian themes seem to have been indispensable to him. Our concern is with Marx's understanding of religion, and here Hegel's influence comes in at a decisive point.

This point is that the God whom Marx was to deny was the God as presented and 'explained' by Hegel. This God was the God who had to be attacked, the most reliable, mature, rational account of God that was available, and once Hegel's God had been disposed of, the major task of criticizing religion would have been done. For Hegel, ultimate reality was rational, mind, Absolute Mind; and what is going on in our world, our universe is a movement or process whereby Absolute Spirit, infinite, eternal, realizes itself by becoming that which it is not – finite, temporal. In a word, this realization takes place in the free creative activity of finite beings, that is to say in the consciousness of man, where the overcoming of alienation takes place, providing freedom for life to overcome all social, religious and philosophical estrangement. In Hegel, there is no clear-cut distinction between God and the world, between the world of Spirit and the world of men: the whole is the world of Spirit. This is, obviously, a massive speculative construction, and the immediate question here is, where does religion fit into it, or more particularly, what is the place of God?

Religion is important for Hegel. It is an area in which estrangement has taken place, in which man externalizes and objectifies. More, it enables man in a state of ignorance or unenlightenment, to glimpse through a veil, as it were, the truth, and more important, to respond to it. In truth, however, the God of religion is but a symbol for Absolute Spirit. It is a necessary symbol for practical purposes for the untutored, unsophisticated who cannot grasp the philosophical truth of Absolute Spirit. Because its understanding of God most nearly approaches the truth, Christianity is the greatest of all religions (and, incidentally, the Christian Prussian State the most advanced realization of the freedom of Absolute Spirit, a point of keenest relevance to Marx). Nevertheless, even Christianity is but an imperfect symbolization of the truth, which can eventually only be arrived at when the religious idea of God is transcended by philosophical understanding. This 'transcendable God', to coin a phrase, is the God whom, or rather which Marx had in mind when he criticized the concept and the religion that accompanied it.[4]

Before coming to Marx's reaction to religion, it is necessary to mention that great intermediary between Hegel and himself, namely Ludwig Feuerbach. A representative of the radical wing of 'Young Hegelians' he early voiced devastating criticism of aspects of Hegel's system. In particular, he did not see why it was necessary for Hegel to bring in at all his idea of Absolute Spirit, so basic to the whole system. This simply meant that Hegel was resting content with abstractions and formal concepts. Feuerbach wanted to get down to basics, not up to speculations. What mattered to him was the solid, the concrete, the here and now, what was available for examination by the senses. Reality is to be found not in Absolute Spirit, but in concrete being, mediated to mankind by sense-perception. 'I differ *toto caelo*', he once said, 'from those philosophers who pluck out their eyes that they may see better.' So, for him, Hegel was not really proving or demonstrating anything with his system: he was merely expounding his own arbitrary concepts. For Hegel, as has been noted, what was ultimately real was mind, spirit, reason. Feuerbach insisted that thinking is something human beings do, it is part of their nature and cannot be elevated above it. 'Absolute Spirit' is not needed to account for anything, let alone man in history. 'Man is what he eats.'[5] Or again, man is only man with other men, the product of man, of culture, and of history.

Feuerbach's main interest for us is naturally his account of religion, and his conversion of theology into what he called anthropology but which today would be more likely recognized as a blend of psychology and sociology. This latter task he accomplished triumphantly in one of the most remarkable books of the century, his _Essence of Christianity_ (1841).[6] Like Hegel, but going far beyond him, Feuerbach saw Christianity as correct in content but mistaken in form. What it discloses in its essence is not truth about God but the essence of man. Hegel had outlined a process of alienation, externalization in religion by which man had pushed, as it were, Absolute Spirit away from him, outside him, on to a remote, totally 'other' God, immune from the changes, weakness and finitude that besets man. Feuerbach takes this much further. God is a focal point for all that has been felt, hoped, dreamed, intuited by man since the human species began. What has happened is a false projection on to an alleged supernatural being. As he put it in another work, God as the epitome of all realities or perfections is nothing other than a compendious summary devised for the benefit of the individual, an epitome of the generic human qualities distributed among men, in the self-realization of the species in the course of the world-history.[7] In other words, what men are doing when they acknowledge God is unconsciously acknowledging the essence of humanity. 'God is an inexpressible sign deep in the souls of men.' God is a vision of humanity which, by thought, can become a revelation of human nature. Man invests God with his own ideal qualities. 'I shew that the true sense of theology is anthropology, that there is no distinction between the predicates [i.e. the qualities we attribute] of the divine and human nature, and consequently no distinction between the divine and human subject.'

Feuerbach can, then, indulge in a massive conversion operation, not merely in principle, but in practice. He considers all the main features of Christian doctrine and converts them into their anthropological (or 'real') equivalent. For example, God is worshipped in the Christian tradition as Trinity: the 'anthropological' sense of this is the recognition of the fundamental nature of the I–Thou relationship; 'God is infinite' really means 'consciousness is infinite'; 'God is love' is but another way of saying 'true humanity is true community'. And so on with the whole range of Christian doctrine, a task which is even now as breathtaking as it is insightful.

Now Feuerbach is by no means saying that religion is a hoax. He is no vulgar despiser. For him, it is above all feeling and it is something which must be gone through. It cannot be dispensed with. Man must externalize himself, or project God in order to come to a correct understanding of his true nature. It is a necessary stage in the development of human awareness. What is more, Christianity is the most perfect form of religion because in it, externalizing or objectifying is carried to the point of demanding its own overcoming. What this means is that in Christianity, the central belief concerns the incarnation of the Word of God in a man, Jesus, God made man in an exclusive, total final way not found in other religions, even in those in which the idea of incarnation is not altogether unknown. For Feuerbach, it is but one step from proclaiming 'God become man' to proclaiming 'man become God', not in the sense of the deification of man but in the sense of realizing that what men were really talking about when they were talking about God ('theology') was not God but the essence of humanity, man ('anthropology'). This step having been taken, all that is necessary now is to have courage to be consistent and to translate theological statements and insights into statements about human possibilities and realities. With the realization that when we are talking about God we are really talking about ourselves, or at least mankind, comes the immense relief of knowing that we do not have to do with some supreme and alien power existing over and above us, threatening, judging and condemning us even as he also protects us: we only have to do with ourselves and our fellows.

This means that the self-alienation involved in religion has at last been truly overcome, there is no longer any need to pretend to be other than we are, responsible to an alien power, unable to change our condition or plan for our future. With this realization comes a tremendous sense of release, of freedom as well, of course, as of responsibility. As far as Feuerbach was concerned, it now became possible as it had never been before to accept 'freedom in community' as man's true nature. How that community is to be realized is not really Feuerbach's question, even though he did say that 'politics must become our religion'. On the whole, religion remained for him the expression of a realm of intimate personal relationships, which, as we shall see, was not nearly enough for Marx. What Feuerbach had done, however, was, vis-a-vis Hegel, to remove the

whole superstructure of Absolute Spirit – as an imaginative but speculative construction which was not relevant to what was going on in
the world, and with it, religion, which he was able to treat as an
aspect of man's understanding of himself. He could present the
proper human milieu as man-in-community, the proper method as
right thinking, the proper goal as human freedom.[8]

With much of this, Marx was able to agree without qualification.
As far as he was concerned, the major philosophical task of understanding what really lay behind religious language, practice and attitudes had been accomplished by Feuerbach – up to a point. But
Feuerbach had stopped short of so understanding the situation as to
be able to transform it. For all his determination to be practical, and
to stick to what could be known by observation, Feuerbach was still
too abstract, one step removed from the real lives of real men and
women in society. Marx himself put it thus:

Feuerbach sets out from the fact of religious self-alienation, the
duplication of the world into a religious and a secular one. His
work consists in resolving the religious world into its secular basis.
But the fact that the secular basis deserts its own sphere and
establishes an independent realm in the clouds, can only be explained by the cleavage and self-contradictions within this secular
basis. The latter, therefore, must be understood in its contradictions and revolutionized in practice. Thus, for instance, once the
earthly family is discovered to be the secret of the heavenly family
the former must itself be destroyed in theory and revolution-
ised in practice.[9]

Marx could sum up in the famous single sentence: 'The philosophers
have only interpreted the world in different ways; the point is to change
it'.[10] From this stand-point, Feuerbach was, of course, to be numbered
among 'the philosophers'. Marx's interest in religion, or rather in
exposing the fallacy of religion, was therefore intensely practical. It
only arose in so far as it was relevant or necessary to understand it and
explain it as it contributed to, or much more likely thwarted, the
progress of society to a freer, juster condition. In other words, he was
only interested in it for the function it had exercised on the past history
of mankind, for the circumstances which gave it birth and nourished it,
and for the creation of conditions that would no longer make it

34

necessary. It was to be explained in terms of his materialist conception of history, and its disappearance was to be looked for as his programme for the achievement of the liberated, Communist society was forwarded. Into the details of his understanding of history in general or of his programme for the future, we cannot enter here in anything like a comprehensive way. Instead, we must take the risk of doing what Marx never did, namely attempt to isolate his thoughts on the origin, functions and future of religion. Even as we do so, we must acknowledge that what he had to say on these subjects was always subordinated, in his thinking at least, to the practical question of how to change the society in which religion flourished.

A lengthy quotation may serve as the basis of exposition of his views on religion. It is from his Introduction to his *Critique of Hegel's Philosophy of Right*:[11]

> Man makes religion, religion does not make man. Religion is indeed man's self-consciousness and self-awareness as long as he has not found his feet in the universe. But man is not an abstract being, squatting outside the world. Man is the world of men, the State, and society. This State, this society produces religion which is an inverted world consciousness, because they are an inverted world. Religion is the general theory of this world, its encyclopaedic compendium, its logic in popular form, its spiritual *point d'honneur*, its enthusiasm, its moral sanction, its solemn complement, its general basis of consolation and justification. It is the fantastic realisation of the human being inasmuch as the human being possesses no true reality. The struggle against religion is therefore indirectly a struggle against that world whose spiritual aroma is religion.
>
> Religious suffering is at the same time an expression of real suffering and a protest against real suffering. Religion is the sigh of the oppressed creature, the sentiment of a heartless world, the soul of soulless conditions. It is the opium of the people.
>
> The abolition of religion, as the illusory happiness of men, is a demand for their real happiness. The call to abandon their illusions about their condition is a call to abandon a condition which requires illusions . . .

The passage continues, making absolutely plain where his own interest in religion lay:

> The immediate task is to unmask human alienation in its secular form, now that it has been unmasked in its sacred form. Thus the criticism of heaven transforms itself into the criticism of earth, the criticism of religion into the criticism of law, and the criticism of theology into the criticism of politics.

Using this text as a jumping-off point, we proceed to consider Marx's understanding first, of the origin and nature of religion, secondly of its function, and thirdly of its future.

Origin and nature of religion

> Man makes religion, religion does not make man. . . . This State, this society produces religion which is an inverted world consciousness, because they are an inverted world . . . religion, as the illusory happiness of men . . .

That religion was an illusion and all religious beliefs both illusory and false, Marx had no doubt. Feuerbach had shown that it was to the 'earthly family' that one must look if one wanted to discover the secret of the 'heavenly family': any credence in the 'heavenly family' in and for itself could only be superstition. But how had the 'heavenly family' ever been believed in in the first place?

Marx seems to give two answers to this question. The first concerns the emergence of the human race from a state of near-animal existence. More precisely, it has to do with the development of human consciousness, and in particular, consciousness of nature, which, as Marx saw it 'first appears to men as a completely alien, all-powerful and unassailable force, with which men's reactions are purely animal and by which they are overtaken like beasts; it is thus a purely animal consciousness of nature (natural religion)'.[12] 'Natural religion', that is, is an animal-like response of ignorance and fear in face of the overwhelming forces of nature which confront the human race.[13] The inference, moreover, is that as men through science and technology understand nature and are able to harness and control it, as it ceased to be 'alien, all-powerful and unassailable', so 'natural religion' will be needed no more, and, as superfluous, will disappear.

The second answer Marx gives to the question of the origin of religion is different but not necessarily wholly unconnected with the first. According to this second answer, religion seems to arise as a reflection in human consciousness of the contradictions of socio-economic life. Such contradictions there assuredly are. According to Marx, they arise through the alienation of man from his work. Instead of producing, of doing work which is his own, which is a genuine expression of himself, man's work becomes alienated, it is not his own, the fruits of it are not his own (as, for example, when he is a slave, or when he works for a wage, the benefits of his toil going to someone else). Out of this basic alienation of man from his work, breaches or distortions in all other relations result – between man and his fellows, between man and nature. Religion can thus be understood, as the expression of a distorted relation between man and nature.

The relationship between man and his work being basic to any understanding of life or 'reality', the key to understanding any society is for Marx the economic base of that society. This is because the economic base of any society is constituted by what in that society men in fact work at and with (the forces of production) and the relations that exist within that society and by means of which such work is done (relations of production). The forces of production thus consist of the tools, techniques, machines and methods currently in use to preserve life; the relations of production consist of the types of social relations which support current forces of production. Examples of such types of relations in different societies would be 'master-and-slave' in the ancient world, 'lord–vassal–serf' in the feudal world, and, of culminating importance for Marx, 'property owner and wage labourer' in contemporary industrial society.

Societies, of course, change. But change in society is brought about not by chance, or by fiat human or divine, but by change in the economic base. Man as producer is paramount, but men do more than produce things. They philosophize, they make and observe laws, they pursue political policies, they paint pictures, write poems and worship. They do indeed have ideas, outlooks, concepts which they seek to express and live by. How are these to be accounted for? They are all, according to Marx, to be understood as the superstructure of society, with no independent existence but, on the contrary, depending on society's real basis, the forces of production and the relations of production. Such ideas, outlooks, concepts change all right, but as part of the superstructure they change as and when the basis or infrastructure changes, for they are in reality a reflection of that. This is so whether men realize it or not. Like legal systems, political systems, every aspect of culture, religion is then part of the superstructure, reflecting the economic basis.

Marx once put it thus:

> In direct contrast to German philosophy [meaning Hegel and his successors] which descends from heaven to earth, here we ascend from earth to heaven. That is, the starting-point is not what men say, what they imagine and what they conceive . . . in order to arrive at embodied men; the starting-point is with really active men, and from this real life-process, the development of these ideological reflexes echoes of this life-process are exhibited. The shadowy forms in the brain of man are the necessary sublimates of their material life-process, which is empirically establishable and linked to material pre-conditions. Morality, religion, metaphysics and the rest of ideology and forms of consciousness corresponding to them, thus no longer retain the semblance of independence. They have no history, no development, but men developing their material production and their material commerce with one another, alter, with this reality, their thought and the products of their thought. It is not consciousness which determines life but life that determines consciousness.[14]

If religion, for example, as part of the superstructure, has no independence of its own but is rather to be understood as a reflection of something in the infra-structure or economic base, one may well ask: of what, then, is it a reflection? Marx's answer would be that in any given society, religion reflects the fact that existing social relations have come into contradiction with existing forces of production. Very much with religious experience and practice in mind, Marx could write further:

> It is self-evident, moreover, that 'spectres', 'Christian bonds', 'the higher being' . . . are merely the idealistic, spiritual expression, the conception apparently of the isolated individual, the image of very empirical fetters and limitations, within which the mode of production of life, and the form of intercourse coupled with it, move.[15]

Following out the implications of this statement, it appears that religion is to be interpreted as an image and reflection of the contradictions in the base of all societies up to and including Marx's own, 'the image of the very empirical fetters and limitations' being the insecurities, the inequalities, injustices and everything in society which prevents men living as free men in a free community, freely enjoying in community the fruits of their labours, with all estrangements (flowing from the basic estrangement of man from his work) overcome. Because it originates, on this argument, from the basic contradictions in society, religion thrives on these contradictions, and will continue to do so until these contradictions are overcome.

As long as it does so, religion performs very important functions in society, and to these we now turn.

Functions of religion

Religion is the general theory of this world . . . its enthusiasm, its moral sanction, its solemn complement, its general basis of consolation and justification . . . The struggle against religion is therefore indirectly a struggle against that world whose spiritual aroma is religion.

Religious suffering is at the same time an expression of real suffering. . . . Religion is the sigh of the oppressed creature, the sentiment of a heartless world, the soul of soulless conditions. It is the opium of the people.

'. . . opium of the people.' This last is Marx's most famous phrase on religion, and it indeed represents his dominant view. Before considering it in detail, however, it is worth noting the phrases which precede it in this passage: '. . . an expression of real suffering . . . the sigh of the oppressed creature, the sentiment of a heartless world, the soul of soulless conditions.' These phrases suggest that religion has a more constructive role to fill than the expression 'opium of the people' on its own indicates. Whatever else religion may have been responsible for – and, of course, it is always illusory – it has stood, according to Marx, for some things not altogether bad. It has, for example, embodied an acknowledgment of real suffering in the world. It has helped people to endure the hardest of lives and the

39

cruelest of conditions by holding out before them the hope, the promise of better things to come – in the next world if not in this. In short, it has at times had a useful consolatory function which has kept people going. Yet it is precisely this consolatory function which, though in some respects beneficial, in most respects constitutes the most dangerous aspect of the illusion which is religion. For by lifting people's eyes up to an alleged blissful future in heaven, it diverts them from the intolerable conditions and injustices of the here and now. It is therefore a diversion from the real task of transforming existing conditions and existing society. More than that: religion is never merely neutral as regards any existing form of society. Being a reflection of it, it almost invariably supports the *status quo*, the establishment, the forces in power. It sanctifies everything it touches, as someone once said, and in Marx's view what it supremely sanctified was the interest, property and privileges of the dominant class.

Marx's analysis of society, already referred to, in which the economic base was the all-important, 'real' feature, had highlighted the significance of the class struggle in history. As forces of production and relations of production changed, so conflict of class interests develop and the antagonisms inherent in society develop. On Marx's reading of history, organized or institutional religion had almost invariably functioned to strengthen the position of the rulers, the oppressors, the exploiters. It had done this by sanctifying their rights, by offering illusory compensation to the ruled, the oppressed, the exploited, and by fostering a spirit among this latter class of compliance, obedience and non-resistance.

How accurate a reading of the history of religion this is will be referred to later, though it is impossible not to admit that there is at least some evidence on which Marx could legitimately base it. One devastating passage he was able to quote from an English churchman makes the point forcibly;

Hunger is not only a peacable, silent, unremitting pressure but, as the most natural motive of industry and labour, it calls forth the most powerful exertions. . . . It seems to be a law of nature that the poor should be to a certain degree improvident, so that there may always be some to fulfil the most servile, the most sordid, the most ignoble offices in the community. The stock of human happiness is thereby much increased, whilst the more delicate . . . are left at liberty without interruption to pursue those callings which are suited to their various dispositions.

The Poor Law, by helping the hungry, 'tends to destroy the harmony and beauty, the symmetry and order, of that system which God and nature have established in the world'.[16] With friends and supporters of Christianity who could speak like that, who needs enemies?

Marx saw religion as always operating to buttress the position of the ruling class. Moreover, he claimed this not as a visionary insight or as a damning indictment of his contemporary society and contemporary church but as the fruit of scientific observation. By unearthing the economic base of a society and the form of distortions evident there he claimed to be able to show a connection between that society and the prevailing religion in it.

For example, he designated the Asiatic, the ancient, the feudal and the modern bourgeois methods of production as so many epochs in the progress of the economic formation of society. To the first of these, there corresponded what he rather vaguely called Asiatic religions, referring generally to either the religions of the Near East or to Hinduism. Corresponding to 'the ancient' mode of production was 'ancient religion', mainly Graeco-Roman religion, though again there was not much precision in his discussion or description of this, or indeed its distinction from Asiatic religions. The religion which went hand in glove with the feudal mode of production in Europe in the Middle Ages was, of course, Roman Catholicism, which acquired its power and supremacy because the economic and social relations of the feudal age required it. As for the fourth method of production, the modern bourgeois method of capitalism, Protestantism came into its own as the appropriate religious expression. 'The religious world', he wrote, 'is but the reflex of the real world. And for a society based upon the production of commodities, in which the producers in general enter into social relations with one another by treating their products as commodities and values, whereby they reduce their individual private labour to the standard of homogeneous human labour – for such a society, Christianity with its cultus of abstract man, more especially in its

41

bourgeois development, Protestantism, Deism, etc., is the most fitting form of religion.'[17] It should be added that despite the close fit between Protestantism and modern bourgeois society, it is in the social and economic circumstances of this last that Judaism comes into its own. For Marx, who was particularly savage in his treatment and analysis of Judaism as a religion, this religion was founded on selfishness, it bred the worldly Jew whose cult was bargaining and whose 'jealous God' was money, whose spirit, moreover, had pervaded modern Protestantism and, in the more economically advanced nations, dominated Christianity.

According to Marx, then, the functions of religion were consolatory, exploitative, and supportive of the currently dominating regime. But what of its future?

The future of religion

The struggle against religion is therefore indirectly a struggle against that world whose spiritual aroma is religion. . . . The abolition of religion, as the illusory happiness of men, is a demand for their real happiness. The call to abandon their illusions about their condition is a call to abandon a condition which requires illusions.

The premise is that religion is an illusion, and the conclusion, based on Marx's analysis of the development of society, is that this illusion has no future. This, it must be said, is entirely consistent. The goal is the classless, Communist society, in which contradictions and alienation in the economic base have been overcome. It is only the persistence of these contradictions and this alienation which preserve and foster the illusion which is religion. When these are overcome, there will be no need for this illusion, religion will, as it were, have no raison d'être, no job, consolatory or otherwise to do. 'The call to abandon their illusions about their condition is a call to abandon a condition which requires illusions.' When that condition is abandoned, as it will be, according to Marx, in the Communist society, the religions of this world, like old soldiers, will simply fade away.

It is interesting, and again consistent, if somewhat surprising, that

42

Marx in attacking religion (by exposing its illusory nature) is not defending or commending atheism as such as a positive position. In a way which curiously anticipates the argument of the logical positivists almost a century later, Marx is bold enough to postulate the ultimate meaninglessness of the question even of atheism:

> Once the essence of man and of Nature, man as a natural being and Nature as a human reality, has become evident in practical life, in sense experience, the search for an *alien* being, a being outside man and Nature (a search which is an avowal of the unreality of man and Nature) becomes impossible in practice. *Atheism*, as a denial of this unreality, is no longer meaningful, for atheism is a *denial of God*, and seeks to assert by this denial the *existence of man*. Socialism no longer requires such a roundabout method: it begins from the *theoretical and practical sense perception* of man and Nature as real existences. It is a *positive* human *self-consciousness*, no longer a self-consciousness attained through the negation of religion, just as the real life of man is positive and no longer attained through the negation of private property (*communism*). Communism is the phase of the negation of the negation, and is consequently, for the next stage of historical development, a *real* and necessary factor in the emancipation and rehabilitation of man ...[18]

Religious belief, then, can be recognized by the enlightened as an illusion now: Marx goes further and heralds a time when both theism and atheism will be seen to be meaningless.

Marx's confidence about the eventual demise of religion as the socio-economic conditions are changed so as to make it unnecessary, carried with it, for him, at least one very important consequence. This concerned the appropriate attitude of the Communist to religions, and, particularly in the European context, to the churches: persecution was neither necessary nor desirable. Although it would be necessary to counteract false teaching on the part of the churches, and although it would be necessary to do away with privileges which served to buttress the authorities of the old and passing order, persecution as such would tend only to stiffen resistance and, in the long run, impede an educated advance. So, as far as Marx himself was concerned, the appropriate attitude for the Communist to adopt towards religion was, in the main, to let it, of itself, simply fade away.

This conclusion of Marx should not be allowed to be obscured by the fact that it has frequently not been adopted by Communist governments. There is, of course, no denying the fact that religious persecution, sometimes of a virulent kind, has taken place and is taking place in certain Communist countries. There is too much evidence available from Russia, for example, or China. Despite theoretical guarantees of the freedom of religious observance, the practical difficulties placed in the way of believers and the sometimes penal disabilities under which they must live if they are unwilling to compromise or deny their beliefs are in many places much too strong to be overlooked. Perhaps, however, Marx should not be blamed for the hard line taken by some of his successors. More than that, contemporary Communist attitudes to religion are by no means uniform. In view of the sharply divergent attitudes taken within contemporary Communism, it is simply not possible to generalize: as regards the churches, what is going on in Russia and China is very different indeed from what is going on in Poland, say, or Hungary or Cuba. In any of these latter countries, the churches do not seem to be continually molested nor openly suppressed.

It is also fair comment that whether there is or is not persecution, the practice of religion under Communism does seem to be taking a far, far longer time to 'fade away' than one might have expected from Marx's confident assertions about the future, or rather the non-future of religion.

This is a convenient point at which to offer a comment or two on the significant features of Marx's account of religion. First, what is to be said of the claim that in origin what he called 'natural religion' was a purely animal consciousness of nature, appearing at first as completely alien, all-powerful, unassailable force? This has been rather savagely criticized on the grounds that it raises severe difficulties of fact, as well as of internal consistency. As far as the facts go, there is little confirmation that animals react to nature as if it were a completely alien thing: animals do not seem to spend their time cowering in the presence of natural occurrences. As for the reactions of the earliest representatives of the human race, there is little evidence to support the conclusion that primitive man found nature to be an alien thing, or that his natural religion was akin to an animal reaction to unassailable forces. On the contrary, some theorists have, on the basis of the evidence available to them, been able to maintain that man's first religious conception, far from being based on feelings of weakness or fear, were characterized by confidence, even joy. The question of internal consistency is raised because Marx does not clearly relate his account of religion as 'animal response' with his account of religion as the reflection in consciousness of the contradictions in socio-economic life. Marx seems to imply that religion in terms of the first explanation is superseded by religion in terms of the second. This not only does not necessarily follow but conceals the more likely conclusion that if Marx had been right about religion as 'animal response' he should have been willing to recognize it as an enduring element in society. Such difficulties have led one not wholly unsympathetic critic to characterize Marx's account of the origin of religion as 'ill-informed and illogical'.[19]

Much more interesting, from the perspective of religion, is Marx's dominant emphasis on religion as something expressing no independent reality but as a reflection in human consciousness of the contradictions of socio-economic life. Marx claimed, it will be recalled, that this was the understanding resulting from a scientific reading of the history of society in the past and the present, but behind this was the assumption that whatever men might have believed in the past or, indeed, in the present, there could be nothing real beyond what could be seen, heard, touched, tasted or smelt. This was the assumption of materialism – an assumption, as we have seen, shared by Freud – and it is an assumption which is unprovable, and unargued for by Marx. Because, however, it seemed self-evident to him (as it seems self-evident to many men and women today), this did not and does not validate its truth. In fact, it is a metaphysical view, which has to take its place with other and different metaphysical views which have been held and are held and whose proponents claim that they are more consistent with their reading of human experience. Marx was, obviously, a man of his time, and in his reaction against the prevailing idealism of his time, he had some valuable and trenchant criticism to make against that whole tradition of which Hegel with his talk of Absolute Spirit realizing itself in society, was the chief exemplar. To see what is wrong with someone else's metaphysic is not the same thing as establishing one's own, and, in Marx's case, no amount of insistence that, as against everyone else, he was being 'scientific' relieved him of the need to establish his own metaphysic, or, as far as God is concerned, his basic assumption – and this he never did.

In any event, Marx's claim to be scientific needs examination. In his own time, it was this claim that was said to distinguish the theory and programme of the Communist Party from that of other socialist groups,[20] and it is this claim which, because of the extraordinary prestige of science, still carries weight in our time. The basis of the claim was that Marx's analysis of society was based on phenomena and experiences which could be verified by appeal to the accessible facts of history. If his analysis had been to the effect that in the development of societies economic factors play a much more vital role than had previously been recognized, influencing directly or indirectly all aspects of society, his claim might have been justified. Once, however, he went beyond this to deduce that by unearthing the economic base of society with the forces and relations of production of which it was composed, *the* key to understanding was to hand, to the exclusion of all other perspectives, he had clearly left the domain of science.

Even more remote from science is the view of the future which emerged from Marx's analysis of how societies change. It was noted earlier that the determinism which characterizes much post-Marx Communist thinking with its iron laws of history leading inevitably to the ushering in of the classless society was not necessarily fully shared by Marx himself. Yet even any prophecy for the future of history, let alone a prediction of what must happen sooner or later, which claims to be based on what has happened in the past can by no means claim to be scientific. It may be insightful, imaginative, more or less informed – but not scientific. Karl Popper puts it thus:

One thing is settled: No kind of determinism, whether it be expressed as the principle of uniformity of nature, or the law of universal causation, can be considered any longer a necessary assumption of scientific method; for physics, the most advanced of all sciences, has shown not only that it can do without such

46

assumptions, but also that to some extent it contradicts them. Determinism is not a necessary prerequisite of a science that can make predictions.[21]

Popper adds in parentheses – and this is very important for a sympathetic understanding of Marx today: 'Marx, of course, cannot be blamed for having held the opposite view, since the best scientists of his day did the same.'

Marx certainly did attempt to be scientific in his examination of the economic base of various societies and cannot be accused of imposing a uniform pattern on the different societies he studied. On the contrary, he warned against this explicitly: 'Thus we see that events of a striking similarity, but occurring in different historical contexts, produced quite different results. The key to these phenomena can be discovered quite easily by studying each of these developments separately, but we shall never succeed in understanding them if we rely upon the *passe-partout* of a historical-philosophical theory whose chief quality is that of being supra-historical.' Nevertheless, while much credit has been and will be given to Marx for stressing so strongly the 'economic' element too easily obscured in any discussion of human affairs, one must be clear that his claims that all social expression and consciousness (including religion) flowed from the economic base was neither grounded nor supported by science. It certainly does not fit those societies which Weber was to draw attention to in which religious ideas actually influenced the economic situation.[22]

It is necessary to stick here to Marx's attitude to and statements about religion, and therefore no comments are offered on Marxist theory in general. It is relevant, however, to add a word about his reading of the history of religions, the function they had performed and his prophecy as to the future of religion. As far as religions in the past are concerned, it will be recalled that Marx claimed to discern particular affinities of certain religions or traditions for certain types of society: 'Asiatic religions' for the early societies of the Middle and further East; Roman Catholicism for the feudal societies of European Middle Ages; Protestantism for the era of bourgeois capitalism, and so on. Such sweeping generalizations are thought-provoking, and in that sense helpful in providing a provisional perspective from which to look at historical problems, but it is impossible to substantiate them from a study of history. To take but one example, Luther, on any account the father of Protestantism, is more than once referred to by Marx with approval for his views on usury. Was it not Luther who said that 'since society hangs the small thief and since, next to the Devil, there is no greater enemy of mankind than the big thieves who are usurers, they ought to be hunted down and beheaded'? [23] Yet it is the religion of Luther that Marx sees as being the most fitting for a bourgeois society. There is both irony and inconsistency here.

Inconsistency, too, of theory with facts when one looks at both the survival and development of the Roman Catholic Church in and throughout the period of bourgeois capitalism. Its vigorous renewal and support, not only in the capitalist world but in socialist societies as well (Poland, for example, or Cuba), surely testify to some major misunderstanding on the part of Marx.

Mention of Poland and Cuba and the active religious situation to be observed there, brings us to consider what has become of Marx's prophecy as to the future of the illusion that is religion – namely that as the contradictions at the base of society are eradicated through socialism leading to Communism, religion, the product of these contradictions, will 'fade away'. One must be careful here. Socialism in Russia is only sixty years old, elsewhere much younger, and it could fairly be said that there has not been enough time for Marx's prophecy to be vindicated or betrayed by history. All one can say, however, is that as far as organized religion in socialist countries is concerned, the situation seems to vary dramatically from country to country (cf. Albania and Hungary, Poland and USSR, Cuba and China), and at any rate such evidence as there is tends to suggest that with the coming of socialism organized religion by no means necessarily begins to wane.

When we consider Marx's analysis of the true functions of religion, it would be unwise to dismiss this too cursorily. That it does have a consolatory function, with its promise and security helping to keep men and women going in intolerable circumstances, helping to keep hope alive, could and should surely not be denied. It would be an extraordinary thing if a religion attracted significant numbers of adherents and did not in some way meet their needs. Consolation, the provision of help to people under difficulties, even people under oppression, personal or social, is not of itself a signal of unreality – unless one accepts a view of reality which rules this out, arbitrarily, from the start.

Similarly, Marx's contention that the consolatory function of religion always works in the interests of the ruling classes or privileged cliques and against the ruled and the underprivileged ought not to be dismissed out of hand. The evidence of history is relevant here, and no one could now assert that the historical evidence is wholly against Marx. Confining ourselves here to the Christian religion, there is indeed plenty of evidence that the ecclesiastical institutions have frequently seemed to fill the precise role Marx gave them in this respect. Every schoolboy has a picture of the Spanish Inquisition as an instrument of terror in the hands of the ruling powers such as to have made of this a historical cliché, and this is no isolated example. Certainly, from the Constantinian era of the Roman Empire in the fourth century onwards – through the church's buttressing of the feudal system in the Middle Ages, the ability of the ruling powers to manipulate the church to their advantage in the birth, growth and expansion of the independent states from the sixteenth century onwards; the failure of established churches to resist or protest effectively against the excesses and miseries caused by the industrial revolution; the connection between the Christian missionary activities of the great European powers and their imperialist expansion in the new worlds of Africa, America and the Far East, even the willingness of certain churches today in the USA and Europe to allow themselves to be exploited by anti-Communist agencies in the interests of sanctifying a crude capitalism – there is indeed plenty of evidence to support the charge that the Christian church has all too frequently acted as a supportive agency of the *status quo*. Certainly, Marx's own experience at the hands of the Christian Prussian state provided him with ample evidence for his thesis.

Yet the question remains whether the historical evidence overall is such as to vindicate Marx's sweeping indictment. His own collaborator, F. Engels, drew attention to the radical potential of Christian faith, hinted at, for example, in the property-sharing community spoken of in the early chapters of the book of Acts (Acts 2.42–47), or

49

in the radical communities of the Reformation, such as that associated with the name of the Anabaptist Thomas Münzer in six-
teenth-century Saxony, urged, in the name of religion, to revolt.
Certainly, it would be possible to multiply instances and to produce
an impressive catalogue of individual Christians, groups and incid-
ents of church history where civilizing, humanizing influences on the
one hand, and calls for justice and the relief of oppression were, on
any reckoning, far more evident than the provision of consolation to
victims of exploitation.[24]

Rather than stage a slanging match of accusation and justification,
it is surely sufficient, in order to question Marx's account of the
principal function of religion, to point out first, that this is by no
means the unanimous verdict of historians best qualified to pro-
nounce; and second, that from the time of the prophets of Israel,
throughout history and certainly in our time, the voices that have
been most critical of the religious institution and its practical concern for justice for the oppressed have been found within it, not
outside it.[25]

If Marx's views on the nature and function of religion cannot, in
the light of experience or logic, be accepted as a total account, the
conclusion must not be drawn that there is no truth in them or help
in them for Christians trying to understand their own faith and their
church. This would be disastrous, for it would be simply false. For
one of the most remarkable features of Christian thought in our time
is its willingness to take seriously Marx's insights.

For a hundred years or so after he first began writing, Communism and Christianity were generally recognized as being at
daggers drawn, representing two mutually exclusive systems between
which the only appropriate attitude was one of open hostility. It is
only, after all, some fifteen years or so since one regularly heard
voiced in Christian circles in Britain and America the slogan 'Better
dead than red!'. Now, however, in many parts of the world, dialogue
between Christians and Communists has become commonplace, and
in some parts of the world, notably in South America, active co-
operation is the order of the day, to the point, indeed, where Fidel
Castro, President of Communist Cuba, could say:

Nobody could love all men and be anti-Marxist in the social meaning of the term ... to be Christian and Marxist in economy, in politics and in all these things, without entering the field of philosophy, which is never debated among us.[26]

This astonishing turn of events forms an intriguing story, with many strands – among them the survival and vitality of churches under the Communist regimes of Eastern Europe; the growing voice of Christians in the Third World, sensitive to what they can only see as capitalist exploitation; the development of various types of Marxism, most of them as embarrassed by certain developments in Soviet Russia as Christians are by the Spanish Inquisition; the realization by Christians in the West that there is nothing sacrosanct about the capitalist system. This story cannot be told here. But it is necessary to give some brief indication of those elements of Marxist thought which are proving highly constructive for Christian thinking.

First, while Marx's thesis that religion is to be wholly understood as an ideological reflection of economic conditions must be rejected, what must not be asserted is that there is no connection between general social conditions, including economic conditions, prevailing at any given period in history and the theological and ethical expressions of religion. As far as Christianity is concerned, that there is such a connection, and an important connection, simply has to be accepted. To say that religion has its own distinctive features which have to be regarded in their own right is not to say that religion exists and is practised in a vacuum, cut off from all other dimensions of life. On the contrary, in Christian terms, no realistic response to the love of God is possible on the part of the community which is the church unless a realistic assessment is made both of the society in which that community is set and of which it forms part and of the practical ways of expressing that response. In our world, many Christians are today finding Marx's analysis of society a considerable resource in attempting just such a realistic witness and mission.

To see this, one need not go the length of Karl Popper, who, for all his criticisms of Marxist theory, concedes that it is no small measure due to Marx's moral reformation that Christianity has changed.[27] One need only look to those contemporary South American Christians who see Marxists as their allies rather than their enemies in their Christ-inspired struggle to express love in terms of justice, freedom, and humanization for the poor, and who see that what has to be fought is not so much the ill-will of evil men as the economic structures which hold them in check. It is not that they accept Marx's dogma that the proletariat has some messianic role to fulfil. It is rather that this dogma has helped them to accept and act upon what has surely been implicit in Christian teaching all along: that Christianity has and must have a bias in favour of the poor and under-privileged, and that love must look at the whole man and woman in society, in their material, physical and social needs, as well as at their soul.

Secondly, Marx's interpretation of history as the history of class struggles has had a very healthy influence on Christian understanding of the church. No Christian theologian would accept that the essential function of the church is to act as an instrument of exploitation in the hands of the ruling class, yet this very contention offers a useful perspective from which to understand much of what has gone on in the church in the past and what is going on there in the present. In Britain, in a period of marked decline in church membership and attendance, there is a great deal of analysis going on with the aim of understanding how to preach the gospel so as to appeal to the industrial working classes. One contention being debated is the extent to which the industrial working classes ever 'belonged' to the church. Certainly, there is considerable evidence that in England and in Scotland in the hey-day of industrial revolution in the nineteenth century, the urban industrial masses were largely estranged from the church. However that may be, few people would now deny that both in its language of worship and in the points of morality it chose to emphasize, the church often represented a strictly middle-class ethos, from which it has by no means yet been liberated. That more and more people are now aware of this, and sensitive to the unfaithfulness to the whole gospel which it reflects, can, for Christians, surely be counted as nothing but gain. It is only right that for much of this, Marx should be given the credit.

Thirdly, mention was made earlier of Marx's development of the concept of alienation as the divorce of man from his work, and as the basic conflict to be overcome if mankind was to be liberated. It would be tempting to equate this concept with the

52

Christian concept of 'sin'. This is not possible. 'Alienation', in Marx's sense, is a technical term of sociological analysis; 'sin' is a theological category, generally meaning 'separation from God', or 'man's abuse of his capacity for self-transcendence', or, more simply, 'that selfishness which prevents man responding as he should toward God and his neighbour'. However sin is expressed, it has, for Christians, a distinctive meaning which cannot be reduced to the separation of man from his work. Nevertheless, what Marx has done for Christian thinking is to emphasize that there is an economic and social dimension to sin which has often been tragically overlooked. For far too long, Christians have been content to think of sin as an affair of individual conduct only: the fact that society could be sinful in its institutions, in the economic structures it considered legal and normal, in the economic powers sanctioned in favour of one group as over against another, was not understood, or if understood, conveniently ignored. In the light of the Marxist analysis, if Christian thinkers and preachers continue to ignore this dimension, they do it without excuse. It is no accident that political and liberation theologies are very much coming to the fore at this time. Marx's analysis offers a considerable resource for anyone interested in probing the perplexities and social pervasiveness of sin.

Finally, it is interesting to note that of all the possible ways open to men and women today to understand the world they are living in, what distinguishes Christianity and Communism is their claim to insight into the future, to offer an answer to the question 'What may we hope for?'. Communism, taking its cue from Marx, hopes for the coming classless society, when humanity will be in a new sense free. Christianity, taking its clue from the teaching of Jesus himself and the church's teaching about Jesus, hopes for the coming in all its fullness of the Kingdom of God, already in some sense inaugurated with the life, death and resurrection of Jesus.

For Marx, the introduction of the classless society, to which all his work was directed, did not represent the end or goal of history as much as its real beginning (when the true potential of men an women in a free society could begin to be realized).

Communism is the plan of negation of the negation, and is consequently the next stage in historical development, a real and neces-

53

sary factor in the emancipation and liberation of man. Communism is the necessary form and the active principle of the immediate future, but communism is not itself the aim of human development in the final form of human society.[28]

He did not ask to see the distant scene, one step, as it were, enough for him. His successors, however, were not so reticent, and the New Programme of the Communist Party of the Soviet Union of 1961 in a section, 'Communism the bright future of all mankind', was rash enough to predict that not long after 1980 the new society would have been achieved. In it, all men's needs will be supplied: they will be free to cultivate all resources, material, cultural, moral; work will be no longer alienated and alienating but voluntary; there will be over-all planning for the benefit of all; there will be no more international rivalry but friendship, co-operation and peace.[29]

Christians' understanding of sin prevents them taking such an optimistic view of the immediate future of mankind. The church has never completely ignored the biblical emphasis on 'the last things' or eschatology, but, despite the spasmodic protests of sects preoccupied with the Second Coming of Christ, it has tended to be more concerned with the hereafter than with the future of the 'here'. An American scholar is prepared to generalize thus: 'The God of orthodox churches has usually been pictured as one most at home in the past, as relating to the present only through the churches and keeping his distance from those revolutionary tendencies in society which accept responsibility for the future and somehow threaten the social status of Christianity. The first generation of Christians were fired by hopes for the kingdom; the second wave of Christianity built the church as an interim device while waiting for the kingdom; later generations identified the two.' He goes on to add: 'Today, the task is to re-activate the Christian hope by pointing to the Kingdom of God, whose biblical images have been blurred in the history of Christianity.'[30]

Christian theologians have been setting about this task with great vigour, and in reinstating 'hope' as a key category of the Christian vocabulary, have gained not a little help from such Marxist scholars as Ernst Bloch. Not that Jürgen Moltmann or Wolfhart Pannenberg or any of the many other contemporary expositors of a 'Theology of

54

Hope', as it is called, would dream of equating the Kingdom of God with the Marxist classless society – they do not and would not. But they have seen that the traditional teaching concerning the Kingdom of God has been heavily overweighted away from concern with the future of society in this world; that authentic biblical insights concerning 'the last things' or eschatology must also involve the future of society, and, more than that, a transformation of society. In this work of bringing hope right back into the forefront of Christian thought, most constructive use has been made and is being made, acknowledged or unacknowledged, of the Marxist model. Marx's challenge, 'the philosophers have only interpreted the world in different ways; the point is to change it', works out in a modern theology of hope as follows: In the interim between the resurrection of Jesus and the final resurrection (however interpreted) the purpose of the church is not merely to interpret the world of history or humanity differently, but in the expectation of the divine transformation to be busy changing it. The essence of Christianity is to kindle hope; the church is the community of God's tomorrow.[31]

Here, as in the other areas mentioned, Marx's teaching is still providing a very healthy challenge to Christians to say more clearly what they mean by the Kingdom of God, to what extent it involves a direct reference to the personal, social and political life of this planet now or is solely concerned with 'otherworldliness', and if it is concerned with life 'here', how it goes beyond the classless society of Marxist teaching. That this challenge is being taken up is one of the most heartening signs of the current scene – and not only for the Christian church. It is one more area in which dialogue between Christians and Marxists is full of constructive promise in the sense of forcing each group to face the difficult and relevant questions the other is asking of it. The traffic is by no means one way. There are indications that Marxists are here and there beginning to admit that Christians have important questions to put to them. In the classless society, will individuals be freely reconciled to one another, will not the fact of death and the fear of death not continue to exert alienating pressures and demand personal responses which cannot depend solely on overcoming the estrangement of man from his work, can mankind really ever dispense with the notion of a transcendence going beyond the scientifically investigable 'facts' of human behaviour and nature? Could Marxists not be even more dialectic in their thinking: instead of sacrificing everything now for the problematic future of the classless society, is there not a humanizing and healthy realism in the Christians' understanding of their hope, that he who is to come is in some sense already here?

These must be left as questions here. The main point is that on their different understandings and attitudes towards the future there is enormous scope for dialogue. As far as Christians are concerned, they need not be afraid of Marx. In so far as he has attempted to 'explain religion and faith away', he has failed. But he has also posed questions and offered perspectives to which many Christians are today able to make a positive, constructive response.

3

EMILE DURKHEIM

1858–1917

A Sociological Explanation

The third classic attempt to explain away religion is that associated with the name of Emile Durkheim, the pioneer sociologist. In some ways it is the most interesting from the point of view of the believer, or the student of religion. For although the concluding contention is that religion relates to no independent reality but is to be wholly understood and explained in terms of something else – in this case 'society' – it is something which, contrary to Freud's view, definitely has a future, and which, contrary to Marx's view, far from being dangerous, is helpful and indispensable. In this case, as against the two others so far considered, 'explaining away' does not mean explaining altogether out of existence, rather explaining without remainder in terms of something else.

Durkheim was a Frenchman, born in Lorraine in 1858. Like both Freud and Marx, he belonged to a Jewish family, of rabbis and rabbinical scholars. He was originally destined for the rabbinate himself. There is a suggestion that, at an early age, under the influence of a Catholic teacher, he had some sort of mystical experience, but the outcome was not to reinforce his Jewish faith or to convert him to Christianity, but to make him profoundly agnostic in matters religious for the rest of his days. The irony of the situation has often been pointed out, that one so totally agnostic should grant religion, as he did, a key role in society.

A serious, not to say grave, boy, dedicated to learning he did brilliantly at school, and pursued his studies at the École Normale Supérieure in Paris. There, although he impressed some of his teachers mightily, he did not distinguish himself overall, and did not get too much intellectual satisfaction. Although he was nicknamed 'The Metaphysician', he was in fact eager to explore and exploit the new scientific spirit which was sweeping through Europe, and he found himself out of tune with the humanistic emphasis still prevalent, with its insistence on Greek verse and Latin proses. (For example, of the two compulsory dissertations required of students, one had to be in Latin. Durkheim did his on Montesquieu.)

When he left the university, he became a teacher, and for five years taught in various French provincial schools. During this time, he was keenly studying the new social sciences which were beginning to flourish in France and Germany, and in 1887 he was appointed to the University of Bordeaux to teach a new course in social science. He remained at Bordeaux for nine years, and it was during this time that he published the major works that were to mark him out as a pioneer sociologist.[1] His next, and last move was to Paris, to a new chair, the first in France in social science, and a professor in Paris he remained until his death in 1917.

His great work on the sociology of religion, *The Elementary Forms of the Religious Life*[2] was not in fact published until 1912. This does not mean that he stumbled on religion or developed an interest in it from a sociological point of view only late in life. There is plenty of evidence that he had been keenly interested in it throughout his professional life.[3] Notably, in 1895 he became interested in the work of the Scottish theologian and ethnologist, W. Robertson Smith (on whose researches Freud, incidentally, was later to found[4]) who had studied the religions of the ancient Semites, and who had pointed to the social origins of religion. From that time on he set himself to study systematically the relation between religion and the social order and the crucial importance of religion in the social order. Certainly, however, the crown of his work on the sociology of religion is *The Elementary Forms of Religious Life*, which has proved itself a seminal work, the influence of which is still to be detected. Although a great deal of work has been done on the sociology of religion since 1912, and although a great many of Durkheim's conclusions are no longer accepted, of the closing section of this work, one commentator has said: 'To read it is to participate in some of the greatest moments in the history of social thought.'[5] Another, writing in 1971, claims that except in certain specialized areas, the subject of sociology of religion 'remains as a whole very much where it was left by Durkheim and Weber'.[6] Such opinions point to the importance of this particular 'dissuader'.

Like Marx, Durkheim, in his approach to religion, started with the assumption that whatever people might think they were doing when they were, for example, worshipping, they could not be relating themselves to God in the sense of any reality which transcended the world of nature and of sense. 'Assuredly, it must be a principle for the science of religion that religion expresses nothing that is not in nature, for every science is concerned with natural phenomena.'[7] Unlike Marx, he refused to write it off as a folly to be eventually discarded by enlightened, free men. So his entire study 'rests on the postulate that the unanimous sentiment of the believers of all times cannot be illusory'.[8] Recognizing that law, morality, scientific thought itself are born of religion and have remained imbued with her spirit, he asks: 'How could a vain fantasy have fashioned human consciousness so firmly, so enduringly?'[9] Granting, then, such a high assessment to religion, he saw it as his scientific duty to explore the origins of religion, to investigate its functions in society and to unearth the reality which it, albeit erroneously, expresses. 'The most barbarous and the most fantastic rites and the strangest myths translate some human need, some aspect of life, either individual or social. The reasons with which the faithful may justify them may be, and generally are, erroneous; but the true reasons do not cease to exist, and it is the duty of science to discover them.'[10]

His scientific presuppositions led him to believe that the appropriate way to proceed would be to study religion in its simplest and most elementary form: if he could get at it, and observe it in this form, he would be entitled to draw conclusions which would be valid for less primitive, more complex and sophisticated forms of religion. Behind this, of course, lay assumptions regarding the nature of evolution, assumptions which will be referred to later. Enough to note here that having looked around for a suitable sample – one sufficiently homogeneous or integrated to make a systematic study possible, one the details of which were sufficiently documented by scientific observers to be reliable, and one which, above all, could be said to embody religion in its most primitive simplicity – he settled on the Arunta tribe of Central Australia. This was a tribe of nomadic aboriginals, whose practices and beliefs were both simple and comparatively uncontaminated but also accessible for research. He was

not a 'field man' himself, examining data at first hand. He was prepared to rely on the best evidence available to him from others.

What he discovered was that units of this tribe wandered about in
isolated groups and came together seldom. When they did come
together, however, in their occasional meetings, something significant happened. Feelings of sociability and well-being came to the
surface. These feelings became ritualized, certain objects became
associated with the rituals and acquired a character of sacredness,
becoming central to their beliefs. These objects were the 'totems',
which were to loom so large in Durkheim's understanding of the
origin of religion. The totems were plants or animals, and, because
of the special status they had acquired, were not to be eaten, or
touched, but respected. The special qualities attending these totems
were not confined to the plants or animals themselves. They were extended to objects bearing the emblem of the totem, and to individuals who took the part of officiants at the rites, and often bore upon
them the totem's depiction. In this way, a whole realm of sacred
things is created and is organized into a system, and is opposed to
the realm of ordinary, non-sacred reality.

Totemism is then acknowledged by Durkheim not as one simple,
primitive religion among many simple primitive religions, but as the
simplest, and, logically and historically, the first. As the common
possession of the clan, it is the totem which actually gives the clan its
identity. In addition to clan totems, there are totems applicable to
individuals and totems applicable to larger groups such as 'phatries'
and matrimonial classes. But the basic application of totemism is
to the clan, giving identity to this group of kindred not based on
consanguinity. Moreover, and most importantly, it gives rise to the
acknowledgment of a certain power or force which the clan
experiences.

Totemism is the religion, not of such and such animals or men or
images, but of an anonymous and impersonal force, found in
each of these beings, but not to be confounded with any of them.
No one possesses it entirely and all participate in it. It is so
completely independent of the particular subjects in which it incar-
nates itself, that it precedes them and survives them. Individuals
die, generations pass and are replaced by others; but this force
remains actual, living and the same. It animates the generations of

60

to-day as it animated those of yesterday and as it will animate those of to-morrow. Taking the word in a large sense, we may say that it is the god adored by each totemic cult. Yet it is an impersonal god, without name, or history, immanent in the world and diffused in an innumerable multitude of things.[11]

In effect, what the Australian aborigines were recognizing was something that existed outside the world of profane things, something which confronted them as an anonymous, impersonal force. Towards this force, is directed belief and worship: it is worthy of both because it inspires a vague feeling that something is there, something which was there before the individual, something which will remain after he has gone, something superior to individuality. What is this 'something'? According to Durkheim, it is none other than the force of society.

In his own words:

In a general way, it is unquestionable that a society has all that is necessary to arouse the sensation of the divine in minds, merely by the power it has over them; for to its members it is what a god is to his worshippers. In fact, a god is, first of all, a being whom men think of as superior to themselves, and upon whom they feel they depend. Whether it be a conscious personality, such as Zeus or Jahweh, or merely abstract forces such as those in play in totemism, the worshipper in the one case as in the other, believes himself held to certain manners of acting which are imposed upon him by the nature of the sacred principle with which he feels that he is in communion. Now society also gives us the sensation of a perpetual dependence. Since it has a nature which is peculiar to itself and different from our individual nature, it pursues ends which are likewise special to it; but, as it cannot attain them except through our intermediacy, it imperiously demands our aid. It requires that, forgetful of our own interests, we make ourselves its servitors, and it submits us to every sort of inconvenience, privation and sacrifice, without which social life would be impossible. It is because of this that at every instant we are obliged to submit ourselves to rules of conduct and of thought which we have neither made nor desired, and which are sometimes even contrary to our most fundamental inclinations and instincts.[12]

In short, society awakens the feelings of the divine, calling forth respect, adoration, devotion.

Durkheim noted the power of religion to take an individual out of himself: when his Australians met together after their wanderings they engaged in religious ceremonies and the effect upon them was exaltation, almost ecstasy. They were given entry into a realm different from that of everyday life, a realm extraordinary and transcendent. What was happening was that they were being drawn out of themselves into participation in the group, the society of which they formed part but which was greater than the individual. From this they derived strength. One of the conclusions which Durkheim was to draw from this observation was that gods are created or religions are stimulated when societies are in a state of exaltation, and he cited the cycle of rituals and celebrations associated with the French Revolution as evidence of this. It would have been in line with his reasoning to see the quasi-religious fervour generated in Germany under the Naxis or in China under Chairman Mao as further corroborative evidence.

Such a reflection naturally raises the question of definition of religion, and we have only delayed it until now in order to give an idea of the general drift of Durkheim's thought. As a good man of science, he does not shirk the question of definition, and offered the following as his own mature understanding:

> A religion is a unified system of beliefs and practices relative to sacred things, that is to say, things set apart and forbidden – beliefs and practices which unite into one single moral community called a Church all those who adhere to them.[13]

The reference here to 'one single moral community called a Church' is interesting as it is not an immediately obvious component of a definition of religion. Durkheim, however, insisted on this as he wanted to make clear his own conviction that religion is an 'eminently collective thing'. He also wanted to distinguish it from magic. Though magic and religion have certain things in common, 'magic takes a sort of professional delight in profaning holy things'.

> There is no Church of magic. Between the magician and the individuals who consult him . . . there are no lasting bonds which make

them members of the same moral community, comparable to that formed by believers in the same god or observers of the same cult. The magician has a clientele and not a Church.[14]

It is also interesting that the definition Durkheim opts for contains no reference to belief in a transcendent god. This is because he wants to include within his definition those systems, such as Buddhism, which though clearly religious in character in fact do not include belief in a transcendent deity.

Working from this definition, Durkheim proceeds to expound the essential components of elementary religious beliefs, their origins, and the principal ritual attitudes and rites, and their significance. Particularly important is his presentation of the functions of religion and it is to this functional analysis that we now turn.

First – and this will be obvious from what has already been said – religion has a *unitive* or *integrative* function. It binds a society together, making it one, and providing indispensable integrative properties and symbols. Religious beliefs and practices 'unite all those who follow them in a single moral community'. For this reason, far from being written off in the manner of the eighteenth-century Enlightenment rationalists and their successors as a superstition to be discarded, religion must have a central role in the study of man. Although the reality behind religion is a social reality, religious belief and practice seems to have been the *sine qua non* of the formation of particular societies.

The unitive or integrative function of religion is not restricted to social systems. One of Durkheim's most startling contributions to the sociology of knowledge was his claim that this function extended beyond the social to intellectual systems as well. The origins of human thought and culture, and even the constitution of the human mind are to be related to religious practice.

At the roots of all our judgments there are a certain number of essential ideas which dominate all our intellectual life; they are what philosophers since Aristotle have called the categories of the understanding: ideas of time, space, class, number, cause, substance, personality, etc. They correspond to the most universal properties of things. They are like the solid frame which encloses all thought. . . . They are like the framework of the intelligence. Now when primitive religious beliefs are systematically analysed, the principal categories are naturally found. They are born in religion and of religion; they are a product of religious thought.[15]

The idea of 'time' serves to illustrate this thesis. 'Time' cannot be conceived initially otherwise than by reference to the processes by which we divide it: years, months, weeks, days and hours etc. We differentiate separate moments and periods. But this private differentiation does not of itself constitute the category of 'time'.

It is an abstract and impersonal frame which surrounds, not only our individual existence but that of all humanity. It is like an endless chart, where all duration is spread out before the mind, and upon which all possible events can be located in relation to fixed and determined guide lines. . . . And in reality, observation proves that these indispensable guide lines, in relation to which all things are temporally located, are taken from social life. The divisions into days, weeks, months, years, etc. correspond to periodical recurrence of rites, feasts, and public ceremonies.[16]

What this amounts to is that without religion, the notion of 'time' would never have entered human consciousness. Moreover, what is true of 'time' is also true of other fundamental categories: space, number, cause, power, classification – these are all of religious origin.

Durkheim does not stop there. Just as the fundamental categories of thought have, through religion, social origins, so science itself is to be traced to the same source. The essential ideas of scientific logic are of religious origin. Certainly, science brings a critical spirit which religion ignores, 'surrounds itself with precautions to escape precipitation and bias', and to hold aside the passions, prejudices 'and all subjective influences'. But such qualifications are not enough to differentiate science from religion. Both pursue the same end, indeed, scientific thought is only a more perfect form of religious thought.[17] For an apostle of the scientific method, imbued with the scientific spirit, this, for religion, is praise indeed.

Nearly all great social institutions similarly have been 'born in religion'. The religious life, then, is 'the eminent form and, as it were, the concentrated expression of the whole collective life'. There is, however, a sting in the tail of Durkheim's conclusion: 'If religion has given birth to all that is essential to society, it is because society is the soul of religion.'[18] To this we shall return. In the meantime, enough has been said to indicate the key function of religion in uniting and integrating social and intellectual life.

A second function of religion is stressed by Durkheim. This is *strengthening*, or *revitalizing* function. In a word, the believer who has communicated with his god is not merely a man who sees new truths of which the believer is ignorant: he is a man who is *stronger*, 'he feels within him more force, either to endure the trials of existence or to conquer them'.[19] Given the social reality of religion, it is not surprising that in religious practice, the believer should share in what is really the power of society. The individual soul is, as it were, dipped in the sources from which its life came in the first place, and this makes it less dependant on physical necessities, more master of itself. What takes place is both a collective renovation and an individual regeneration. Through religion, social power is tapped, for the benefit of both the society and the individual. Of course, in participation in the cult, the believer does not know what is actually going on. He feels himself raised above the miseries of the world, above the conditions of being a mere man: he believes he is saved from evil, whatever form he may think evil to take, the first article of every creed being, according to Durkheim, salvation by faith.[20] The source of this strength is not what believers, in the world's different religions, have believed it to be: the objective cause of the sensations believers receive in religious practice is none other than society.

It is necessary to stress the point that the strengthening function of religion is not restricted to the individual. Society itself is also the beneficiary of the succour and refuge religion provides. This is what Durkheim means when he says that the cult is as important to the gods as it is to men, the gods being a manifestation or personification of society. The gods cannot do without their worshippers any more than the worshippers can do without their gods. Translated scientifically, this is another way of saying that society, symbolized by the gods, cannot do without individuals any more than individuals can do without society.

Among other functions which, according to Durkheim, religion

65

exercises in society, two only need brief mention, a *disciplinary* function and a *'euphoric* function'. As might be expected, he traces the origins of morality or the rules of behaviour which any given society observes back to religion and sees religion as promoting the discipline necessary for social life. Like Freud, he recognized that society perforce imposes certain demands on its members as to what conduct is acceptable and what is not. No society can function without the recognition by its members of certain necessary restraints and controls. Religion makes such demands, imposes such restraints and controls, and, moreover, bases them on an absolute demand from beyond, from a different sphere from the sphere of everyday living, and in so doing creates a healthy, disciplined community. Although the sanctions it provides are basically social sanctions, they do not appear to the worshipper as such: they go beyond the mere wishes of society. In this way, they effectively enable people to live together in community.

By 'euphoric function' is meant here the ability of religion to generate pleasant feelings of social well-being. It can and does have, in addition to moral fruits, elements that are genuinely aesthetic and recreational, which add to the feeling of comfort which the worshipper, for example, draws from the rite performed.

> After we have acquitted ourselves of our ritual duties, we enter into the profane life with increased courage and ardour, not only because we come into relations with a superior source of energy, but also because our forces have been re-invigorated by living, for a few moments, in a life that is less strained, and freer and easier. Hence religion acquires a charm which is not among the slightest of its attractions. . . . This is why the very idea of a religious ceremony of some importance awakens the idea of a feast.[21]

This euphoric function is of special significance in times of trouble or distress. Death is the obvious example. When a member of a family group dies, the group feels itself threatened, lessened. To react against its sense of loss, it assembles together, individuals tend to seek one another out and to renew collective sentiments. The cult enables those involved to express certain feelings and emotions together. In this way, the group is in fact not weakened. Communication, even in sorrow, takes place, and every communion of mind, in whatever form it may be made, raises the social vitality. This, then is yet another way in which religion constructively serves society.

Given, on the one hand, the enormous positive value which Durkheim, on the basis of his scientific researches, places on religious belief and practice, and given, on the other hand, his unearthing of the social basis, the power of society, which lies behind it, it becomes a critical question to ask what Durkheim sees as the future of religion. Here he stands in stark contrast to both Freud and Marx. For these two, religion had no future, rendered, as it would be, superfluous in the one case by insight into individual and group psychology, and in the other, by transformation of society's economic base. For Durkheim, religion definitely has a future. Society cannot flourish without it. The secret, the soul of religion has been discovered by science to be society itself, and, of course, science reigns supreme. Yet there is something 'eternal' in religion which makes it necessary to life.

To this high assessment, however, an important qualification has to be made. There can now be no going back on science.

> From now on, faith no longer exercises the same hegemony as formerly over the system of ideas we continue to call religion. A rival power rises up before it, which, being born of it, ever after submits it to its criticism and control. And everything makes us foresee that this control will constantly become more extended and efficient, while no limit can be assigned to its future influence.[22]

Religious thought, in other words, must progressively retire before scientific thought as the latter becomes more fitted to the task of explaining more and more of the natural world. What this means in practice is far from clear. The best clues to Durkheim's meaning are perhaps to be found in those two elements which he describes as eternal in religion, the cult and the faith.

As far as the cult is concerned, he cannot envisage a society which does not need to uphold and re-affirm at regular intervals collective feelings and ideas which give it its unity and its personality. This can only be done by means of reunions, assemblies, meetings, ceremonies 'which do not differ from regular religious ceremonies, either in their object, the results which they produce, or the processes employed to obtain these results'. For him, there is no essential difference between 'an assembly of Christians celebrating the principal dates of the life of Christ, or of Jews remembering the exodus from Egypt or the promulgation of the decalogue, and a re-union of citizens commemorating the promulgation of a new moral or legal system, or some great event in the national life'.[23] He grants that it is not easy to envisage what the feasts and ceremonies of future society will be like. This is because society is in a state of transition, not to say confusion. Yet he is sure things will change.

A day will come when our societies will know again those hours of creative effervescence, in the course of which new ideas arise and new formulae are found which serve for a while as a guide to humanity; and when these hours shall have been passed through once, men will spontaneously feel the need of reliving them from time to time in thought, that is to say, of keeping alive their memory by means of celebrations which regularly re-produce their fruits.[24]

So much for the cult. As regards 'faith', this is above all an impetus to action, which science cannot supplant. For faith provides a theory of reality to live by. 'Science is fragmentary and incomplete; it advances but slowly and is never finished; but life cannot wait. The theories which are destined to make men live and act are therefore obliged to pass science and complete it prematurely.'[25] — Religious speculation, then, cannot be dispensed with altogether. Based, however, as it is, on 'the obscure intuitions of sensation and sentiment', it must in the future acknowledge this. It can claim and exercise the right to go beyond science, but it must begin with a humble admission of what is going on, willingly submitting to science's criticism and control.

For Durkheim, then, religion is a reality, with a present which is undeniable and useful, a past which is positively honourable, and a future which, if not exactly rosy, is still a future. But the secret of religion, its soul, its object is not what the worshippers believe it to be. All is to be understood and explained without remainder in social terms, as society in disguise. So, despite his positive assessment of the role of religion and the future of religion, his reduction, by the effective elimination of God or any transcendent reality, is as all-embracing as that of either Marx or Freud. This is not to say that his researches and far-reaching, bold conclusions have to be accepted or rejected in their entirety. 'Rarely', writes one commentator, 'has religion been so emphatically served as by this anti-clerical, agnostic, positivist mind!'[26] One is inclined to agree, and hopefully the extent of this service will presently emerge. It is necessary, first, to indicate some of the more important criticisms that have been advanced against this daring thesis and the arguments by which it was supported. Such criticisms concern, in the first instance, his method and its presuppositions, his definitions and his conclusions.

First, as regards method, he embarked on his case study of the Australian aboriginal tribe with the assumption that here the essentials of religion would be revealed in their simplest, most primitive form, and that from evidence there unearthed, conclusions of a universal nature could validly be drawn. Another way of putting this would be to say that he used a case study of one people as 'confirmation' of his theory of the nature of religion, and such a procedure, however intensively his study was carried out, would now have to be pronounced unscientific, which would be an ironic judgment on one who set so much store by science and its method.

This apart, Durkheim's particular evolutionary perspective has been widely questioned. There is no universal agreement among social anthropologists or ethnologists that the totemism of the Arunta does represent the simplest and most primitive form of religion,[27] and the whole concept of totemism has been queried. It is therefore not surprising that considerable objection has been taken to the assumption that all religions have evolved from this basic pattern, that the roots of all religion are to be found here.

Durkheim's definition of religion raises a number of problems. It was, it will be recalled: 'A religion is a unified system of beliefs and practices relative to sacred things, that is to say, things set apart and forbidden-beliefs and practices which unite into one single moral community called a Church all those who adhere to them.' One difficulty here is the width of the definition. It has already been noted[28] that Durkheim saw no essential difference between a Christian or Jewish celebration and a reunion of citizens commemorating some great event in the national life. Similarly, in terms of religious symbols, there would seem for him to be no essential difference between, on the one hand, a cross, a candle or a phylactery, and on the other, a flag, a swastika, a hammer and sickle, the club scarf of a football club or even, in Scotland at least on Burns' night, a haggis. Now it is true that a satisfactory definition of religion is notoriously difficult to arrive at. Yet the fact that Durkheim's definition lets in so much in the way of behaviour, symbolism and loyalty that would not normally be recognized or characterized as religious is surely a grave deficiency. There is an essential difference between a Christian making his Easter communion and a Scotsman attending a St Andrew's Day rally or party. There is an essential difference between a crucifix and a swastika. And the difference is that the realities to which they point are of a completely different order.

Implicit in Durkheim's treatment is the assumption which comes through in the definition, that where there is ritual, there is religion, indeed that religion arises from ritualism. The most extreme ritualistic formalism can exist without investing a situation with a religious character. Mention of the proceedings in a court of law, or in Parliament, a university graduation or the closing act of the Trades Union Congress is surely enough to make the point. The truth is that ritual may surround any field of behaviour and of itself does not give rise to religion, any more than it gives rise to art.

Of his conclusions, perhaps the most important was his discovery of the essential functions which religion performed in and for society. It was these which validated religion for him. The question has rightly been asked, however, whether he has not given too passive a role to religion. All the functions he mentions (unitive, revitalizing, euphoric, disciplinary) are basically conservative functions. They serve existing society, but mainly by giving it stability. Though differing from Marx in most respects, here he resembles him in seeing religion as strengthening an existing society by maintaining the *status quo*. But societies, as he was well aware, change. They are dynamic, they do not remain the same. How is religion related to such changes? Durkheim did in fact have a theory of development in society, but this was unrelated to the role of religion. His theory certainly does not fit those cases in which religion does not merely reflect and conserve society but actually causes change. Another eminent sociologist, Max Weber, was prepared to argue

70

that not only did religious doctrines and practice render the behaviour of individuals and groups intelligible: religious conceptions are actually a determinant of economic behaviour and consequently one of the causes of economic change. Weber was prepared to illustrate this by tracing the relation between the spread of the Protestant (mainly Calvinist) work ethic (with its particular interest in predestination, work, saving or thrift) and the establishment (though not necessarily the functioning) of the capitalist regime. Here, religious motivations were among the real factors favourable to dramatic social change.[29]

This suggests that the relation between religion and society is not just as Durkheim envisaged it. This question can be pursued further by asking more precisely concerning the reality to which religion bears witness and which in religion is worshipped. It is, he says, society, but is it actual, concrete tangible society itself or is it some idealization of it? If it is the latter, then it would be more consistent to say not that society accounts for the notion of the sacred, rather that it is the notion of the sacred that transfigures society, as it can transfigure any other reality. Durkheim is aware of the difficulty here and tries to solve it by claiming that to contrast an ideal society with an existing society is to contrast false abstractions. Societies require and have ideals of themselves. 'A society can neither create itself nor re-create itself without at the same time creating an ideal. . . . The ideal society is not outside of the real society; it is part of it.'[30] Therefore, the reality that lies behind religion is the actual society with its own ideals of itself. But it is precisely this claim that creates difficulties as far as the worshipfulness of the object of religion is concerned and have led some critics to reject Durkheim's conclusion. According to Raymond Aron,

> It seems to me absolutely inconceivable to define the essence of religion in terms of the worship which the individual pledges to the group, for in my eyes the essence of impiety is precisely the worship of the social order. To suggest that the object of the religious feelings is society transfigured is not to save but to degrade that human reality which sociology seeks to understand.[31]

Durkheim's understanding of religion stands, of course, in the sharpest contrast with those views which stress the individual's relationship with his God. One thinks here of Kierkegaard, for whom the man of faith must be utterly and entirely alone,[32] or of Whitehead, who once described religion as 'what the individual does with his own solitariness'.[33] Without attempting to adjudicate this debate, it is certainly true that by stressing so completely the group or collective nature of religion, Durkheim runs the risk of effecting the total submergence of the individual, so distorting one of the most widely recognized features of religion.

In particular, it is difficult to see how, on his theory, the religious rebel, or the prophet, or the non-conformist conscience is to be wholly accounted for. How does it cope, for example, with the man who through religious insights sees a higher and more holy justice than his society or his church recognizes, with an Amos or Isaiah, or Jeremiah or Hosea, to illustrate from only one tradition? Are these to be written off as non-religious figures, rather than as the pioneers of religion which they have traditionally been recognized to be? Durkheim broaches this question by admitting the emergence of the 'individual cult', but insists that 'the religious forces to which it addresses itself are only the individualized forms of collective forces'. The religious strength by which an individual is energized cannot come from within him, and there is only one source from which it can come: society. Durkheim's presuppositions come here forcefully to the surface. 'The only source of life at which we can morally re-animate ourselves is that formed by the society of our fellow beings; the only moral forces with which we can sustain and increase our own are those which we get from others.'[34] This, however, is a solution more circular than satisfactory.

The authority of the prophet in his own times and for later times cannot be so easily explained. The theory might, conceivably, fit a closed, static society, but it cannot be applied without a great deal of strain to those societies in which religion is understood to be not merely a prop to social conventions but as a prime agent in changing them. If religion is basically a support for the existing order of society, then the more a man questioned and criticized that society, the less strongly he would rely on religious conviction, the less benefit, support, or succour he would derive from his faith. Yet the prophetic conscience in the Judaeo-Christian tradition – and this is certainly paralleled in other religions – in rebelling, criticizing, acting for a juster order, a more loyal obedience seems to derive from religion not merely support but maximum encouragement. The believer, in his better moments, knows that to walk with God may well involve the risk of rejection to a greater or lesser degree by his own people.

Allied to this question is Durkheim's apparent inability to deal satisfactorily with the 'group-transcending range' or 'universal reach' of the religiously informed conscience. The society for Durkheim is not mankind as a whole (which is not a subject for sociology): it is a specific clan, tribe, country or nation. Yet the God witnessed to in the Old and New Testaments, for example, is the Creator and Father not just of this or that people or tribe but of all mankind, without exception, who summons believers to stretch their imagination and compassion beyond the bounds of tribe and nation to embrace all nations, including those who might be considered their enemies. How, on Durkheim's theory, can this be? To be sure, he does attempt to account for 'the universalistic character of certain religions'. This is to be understood as the natural consequence of increased acquaintance and increased communication between previously isolated communities. International deities are the creation of international social intercourse.

> If sacred beings are formed which are connected with no geographically determined society, that is not because they have an extra-social origin. It is because there are other groups above those geographically determined ones, whose contours are less clearly marked: they have no fixed frontiers, but include all sorts of more or less neighbouring and related tribes. The particular social life thus created tends to spread itself over an area with no definite limits. Naturally the mythological personages who correspond to it have the same character; their sphere of influence is not limited; they go beyond particular tribes and their territory. They are the great international gods.[35]

This is intriguing, to be sure, but implies a degree of international communication which would be hard to substantiate from the history of religions, so hard as to render the theory implausible.

Sufficient reasons have now been advanced to suggest that for all his ingenuity and originality, Durkheim has failed in his attempt to explain away religion in sociological terms. As one sociologist has written, the result has been not, as Durkheim intended, to explain religion, but to explain society.[36]

Yet if this conclusion is accepted, it would be disastrous if Durkheim were to be written off as of no relevance to those trying to understand religion in general or their own religion in particular. Here was a great thinker who, even in the act of attempting to explain religion away, was determined to preserve what he considered to be the reality of religion. Here was a pioneer in sociology concentrating his researches and insights on the phenomenon of religion, and in so doing opening up a rich, new perspective from which to understand it. In a sense he rehabilitated religion as an integral, essential feature of society, so that it could no longer be written off *in toto* as a superstitious hangover from a primitive, unenlightened age, challening all who would try to understand a society to ignore religion, its nature and functions, at their peril.

Confining comment to the case of the Christian religion, it cannot be denied that the churches have fulfilled many of the functions in society which Durkheim indicated. They should not want to deny this. What Durkheim in particular and sociologists in general have forced Christians to see is that the church cannot be understood in splendid isolation from the society in which it is set but only as part of that society and in the context of that society. The Christian life can never be lived and the gospel is not and never has been preached *in vacuo*. It can only be preached at a particular time and in a particular place, and this means in a particular society. This in turn means that only when the realities of that society are understood and taken seriously – and what these realities are it is the job of sociology to discover – can the gospel be effectively preached. This has consequences affecting every area of the church's life, but it will be sufficient by way of illustration to refer to two areas, its theology and its mission.

It is no secret that in the Western world, theology generally cuts little ice as far as the dominant culture is concerned. To the average man or woman – and this, alas, includes the average man or woman in the pew – theology seems to be at best an arcane discipline for specialists only and at worst the dark speculations of those who live

74

at several removes from anything they could recognize as reality. One reason for this is that for too long theologians have been reluctant to understand or take account of the realities of the society in which they work. Among these, perhaps the most important is the language of that society. Theology, of course, needs its technical terms, but the history of theology shows that it has been at its most effective when its technical terms bear some relation, preferably a direct relation, to the terms understood in society at large.

One example would be the doctrine of atonement, the doctrine which attempts to explain the once-for-all significance of the death of Christ. In an age when society was dominated by belief in spirits and demons, the presupposition of its medicine as well as of its meteorology, the significance of Christ's death was most effectively presented as his victory over the demons and all the powers of darkness. In the feudal ages every feudal superior was entitled to 'satisfaction' from his vassal for any infringement of his rights, satisfaction being something over and above what was due, given for an affront to the dignity of the superior. In those ages, the significance of the cross was very well understood as the 'satisfaction' paid by Christ on man's behalf to God for the offence to God of man's sin. However effective these terms were in their own time, there can be no doubt as to their ineffectiveness now: 'satisfaction' has no intelligible technical meaning, and 'victory over the demons' leaves all but the most superstitious cold. What contemporary concepts can do the job which these older ones once did? Some would suggest 'reconciliation', as having a very clear application in a society characterized by divorce; perhaps live notions from the world (always with us) of industrial relations might be drawn into theological service: 'settlement', 'bonus', 'management'. However that may be, what is clear is that unless the theological vocabulary is related to society's own vocabulary, it will not communicate.[37]

The other illustration concerns the church's understanding of its mission. It is largely the development of sociological insights and the growing appreciation of the relation between religion and society which has accounted for a major switch this century in the attitude of the established churches to peoples and societies of other religions. Words like 'heathen', or 'benighted' or 'invincible ignorance'

75

no longer characterize the language of overseas mission. Where once the motive was the saving of souls from perdition and the Christianization of society was synonymous with the Westernization of society, the aim now is much more one of service and sharing in love, and a new respect has grown up for ancient non-Western cultures and traditions. The result is that in Africa, Asia and South America, the churches are not only succeeding in divesting themselves of the damaging taint of being 'Western' institutions (with colonial associations) but demonstrating a vitality and growth which is or should be an inspiration to the older churches of the West. As far as the Western churches themselves are concerned, the major problem they have to face is that of secularization, which has made of the once nominally Christian countries of the West mission territories at home. They can only hope to do this effectively by accepting the realities of what this process of secularization is, of how it expresses itself in society. They are discovering that the task of preaching the gospel in a secular society cannot be realistically tackled without the aid of sociological analysis.[38] This is why in the rapidly expanding situation of new towns in Britain, for example, the hard-pressed ministerial teams avidly seek the help of sociologists to provide an effective analysis of the new society the inhabitants form.

It is, in short, hardly possible to overestimate the service which sociology can render the church in enabling it to understand itself better – for the church after all, whatever else it is, is a society of human beings – and to arrive at an accurate understanding of the wider society in which it is set. The sooner the church as a whole accepts this and acts on it, the better for it. As a pioneer of sociology in general and of sociology of religion in particular, Emile Durkheim indeed deserves credit. In so far, however, as he went beyond an investigation of the functions of religion in society to draw conclusions which effectively so identified religion with society that its object (put plainly, God) as an independent reality was simply denied, he exceeded the legitimate bounds of his discipline, he became of religion not a friend, but a foe. It has been necessary to try to show that his reduction of religion can by no means be accepted as the 'scientific' fact which he claimed and which has consciously or, more likely unconsciously, been received as the 'conventional wisdom' of the day. The object of this exercise would, nevertheless, be defeated if the result were in any way to deter believers from constructively appropriating all possible help that sociology can legitimately offer.

POSTSCRIPT

The explanations of religion considered in this book have been confined to those emanating from the nineteenth and early twentieth centuries which accept religion as a fact but which account for it as a reflection of some non-religious reality, psychological, economic or social. God, as the subject of religion, is denied from the start, but religious language and practice is meaningful in the sense of being translatable into other, non-religious terms. The contention has been that these are the kind of explanations which, in the name of science, are assumed in the popular mind to have satisfactorily disposed of religion, so that it can now be taken for granted that religion in its own right does not require to be taken seriously by the average, intelligent Western man or woman. The conclusion is that when examined, none of these attempts can be said to have wholly succeeded.

These are, of course, illustrations only which do not exhaust the field. Another form of explanation which has unquestionably had its impact is that provided by Logical Positivism, whose best known representative in the English-speaking world was Professor A. J. Ayer, with his explosive and brilliant little book, *Language, Truth and Logic*,[1] which was published in 1936. The fact that he has now changed his mind on many of the arguments there presented has not prevented these arguments having an enormous influence in the middle decades of this century, not least on popular assumptions. Unlike the explanations we have considered, this approach claims to show that religious statements (as well as moral statements and aesthetic statements) are neither true nor false but meaningless. The reason for this is that they are incapable of verification or falsification by reference to sense experience. The details of this claim, along with assessment of its scope and limitations, have been widely examined and can be followed up elsewhere. Yet while it can fairly be shown to have failed in 'disposing' of religion, its influence in theology has been and continues to be both healthy and constructive. It has forced theologians to pay much more attention to the language they use, and it has validly raised the whole question of 'what counts for evidence' in the claims of religion.[2]

From the three explanations with which we have here been concerned and which seem to be of a kind, can any general conclusions be drawn?

First, regarding continuing impact, it is interesting to compare Freud, Marx and Durkheim. As far as Freud is concerned, psychological reductions will remain, but because Freud's star seems to have fallen in his own discipline, it might be reasonable to assume that his speculations outside his particular discipline (and these would include his speculations about the origin, nature and future of religion) will also, in popular influence, eventually wane. Sociology of religion has taken up and developed many of Durkheim's conclusions, but repudiated many more, with the result that his claim that the reality behind religion can be satisfactorily understood as 'society' will also carry less and less authority. Because, however, the close connection which he successfully established between society and religion has emphatically not been repudiated, his impact, not on the disposal but on the relativizing of religion may be expected to continue.

By 'relativizing' is meant here the implication that as societies differ, so religious beliefs and practices must differ. This in turn implies that no society has a monopoly of truth in religion, and that therefore the most that can be said of any particular religion is that it is *relatively* true. This seems to be in direct conflict with absolute claims of Christianity, for example, and one can see here one of the key questions for theology in our time, namely, the relation of Christianity to other religions.

As for Marx, because his avowed aim was not 'to interpret the world but to change it', the long-term impact of his explanation will depend on the success or failure of Marxism as a socio-economic system. This in turn may depend on the ability of religions to disprove in credible practice that they are necessarily instruments in the hands of the ruling classes and guardians of the *status quo*. For Christianity, this will generally mean that the ball is at the churches' feet to provide the evidence that they are not necessarily imbued with the particular values of a particular class, nor inextricably tied to a particular (e.g. capitalist) economic structure.

Secondly, as regards reductions in general, the three forms that have been considered invite the conclusions that the spin-off from reductions of religion is at least as encouraging as the original claim is menacing. That the original claim of these three examples is menacing to the Christian faith cannot be disputed. In an age mesmerized by scientific achievement, the appeal to scientific backing, even though now seen to be an illegitimate appeal, proved irresistibly attractive, capable of absorption at the level of popular assumption. Perhaps it would not have been found irresistible if those who succumbed to it had been enabled to understand better what remained of their faith, to see that Christian doctrine could be expressed in terms which struck a chord with their everyday life, which were not in conflict with scientific endeavour, that Christian practice was not to be exhausted by the routine observance of certain rites. Certainly, it is considerations such as these which will determine the extent of the menace in the future of these and other explanations of religion that will come to the fore.

Once, however, the original claim ceases to be menacing, the constructive potential can also be appreciated. There is no need to repeat the many ways in which Freud, Marx and Durkheim have, ironically perhaps, helped. For those who have been prepared to listen, attentive to truth wherever it may appear, they have provided resources which are still proving invaluable to Christians in understanding better what they believe and in realistically conducting their lives and expressing their hopes in a way which is more consistent both with what they believe and with what is actually going on in their world, their society and themselves. Christianity cannot claim exemption from challenge, even if it wanted to. But should it want to? Every challenge contains within it more than menace: a response in faith demands more than defensiveness, hostility, retreat to fixed positions. It demands an eye for the new opportunity of imaginative compassion that is being offered and an ear for the new word of understanding that is being spoken. We may badly need a modern doctrine of providence, but that God moves in a mysterious way should evoke no surprise. Neither should the admission that to those with eyes to see and ears to hear he can speak through those who deny him.

NOTES

Introduction – 'What everybody knows' (pp.1–9)

1. Technically, of course, there is no guarantee. But if I turn up and there is no seat, I shall legitimately be extremely angry.

2. Antony Flew, *The Presumption of Atheism and Other Essays*, Elek/Pemberton 1976, pp.13 ff.

3. See for example, Vernon Pratt, *Religion and Secularisation*, Macmillan 1970, and its useful bibliography. Also Owen Chadwick, *The Secularization of the European Mind in the Nineteenth Century*, Cambridge University Press 1975.

4. Not all. It must be acknowledged that some Christians will insist on a literal interpretation of the early chapters of Genesis and reject any theory of evolution which would seem to question their biblical understanding. Many more Christians in fact accept some kind of evolutionary theory but think that they are supposed, as Christians, to reject it – a very sad state of affairs and an appalling indictment of timid teaching from the pulpit and in Sunday schools.

Chapter 1: Sigmund Freud (pp.10–27)

1. See Ernest Jones, *The Life and Work of Sigmund Freud*, Penguin Books 1964

2. Ibid., p.138

3. Ibid., p.168

4. S. Freud, *The Interpretation of Dreams*, ET, Allen & Unwin 1955

5. Ernest Jones, *The Life and Work of Sigmund Freud*, pp.299 ff.

6. Konrad Alt. Ibid., p.385

7. In fact, he had his way. Religious ceremonial was kept to a minimum!

8. His views are worked out in *Totem and Taboo* (1918), ET, Routledge & Kegan Paul 1965, where he leant heavily on secondary anthropological sources such as Sir James Frazer's *The Golden Bough* and *Totemism and Exogamy*, and W. Robertson Smith's *The Religion of the Semites*.

9. It is worth noting that not only the beginnings of religion are to be found here. According to Freud, ethics, society and art have their beginnings here as well.

10. S. Freud, *Totem and Taboo*, pp.217–220

11. S. Freud, *The Future of an Illusion*, (1927) ET, Doubleday 1964

12. See in particular, B. Malinowski, *Sex and Repression in Savage Society*, Kegan Paul 1927.

13. Allegedly, Archbishop William Temple.

14. Quoted in H. H. Farmer, *Towards Belief in God*, SCM Press 1942, p.178

15. S. Freud, *The Future of an Illusion*, pp.49f., 60, 86f.

16. See William James, *Varieties of Religious Experience*, (1901–2), Fontana Books 1962, particularly p.39 and pp.321ff.

17. For studies which draw conclusions from Freudian insights rather different from those Freud drew and certainly more compatible with an interpretation of religious belief which does not have to write it off as illusory, see, e.g., Ian Suttie, *The Origins of Love and Hate*, Kegan Paul 1935 and R. S. Lee, *Freud and Christianity*, James Clarke 1948.

18. L. W. Grensted, *Psychology of Religion*, Oxford University Press 1952, p.16

19. Paul Ricoeur, in Alasdair MacIntyre and Paul Ricoeur, *The Religious Significance of Atheism*, Columbia University Press 1969, p.98. 'As a symbol it would be a parable of the ground of love; it would be the counterpart, in a theology of love, of the progression which led us from a mere resignation to Fate to a poetic life. Such, I believe, is the religious significance of atheism.' See also Paul Ricoeur, *Freud and Philosophy*, ET, Yale University Press 1970.

20. See G. S. Spinks, *Psychology of Religion*, Methuen 1963

21. See H. A. Williams in *Objections to Christian Belief*, Constable

1963, pp.35ff. Also *The True Wilderness*, Constable 1965, Fontana edition 1976

Chapter 2: Karl Marx (pp.28–56)

1. Robert Payne, *Marx*, Simon & Shuster 1968, pp.31f., quoted by Delos B. McKown, *Marxist Critiques of Religion*, Martinus Nijhoff 1975, p.15

2. D. B. McKown, op. cit., p.16

3. K. Marx, *Towards the Critique of Hegel's Philosophy of Right*, Introduction

4. This necessarily simplified summary of Hegel's understanding of God should not be allowed to obscure his genuine insight and originality, not least on the social grounding of religious estrangement or alienation.

5. In the original German, this comes out as a pun 'Der Mensch ist was er isst'.

6. First published in English, in the remarkable translation by Marian Evans (George Eliot) in 1854. ET, Harper 1957

7. See L. Feuerbach, *Philosophy of the Future*, quoted in J. Richmond, *Faith and Philosophy*, Hodder & Stoughton 1966, p.73

8. See Alasdair MacIntyre, *Marxism and Christianity*, (revised edition) Duckworth 1969

9. K. Marx, *Theses on Feuerbach* no. iv (1845), in T. B. Bottomore and M. Rubel, *Karl Marx, Selected Writings*, Penguin Books 1970, p.83

10. Ibid., *Thesis* no. xi, p.84

11. K. Marx, *Towards the Critique of Hegel's Philosophy of Right*, see Bottomore and Rubel, p.41

12. K. Marx and F. Engels, *The German Ideology*, see Bottomore and Rubel, p.86

13. When Marx was writing, evolutionary theory was still very much undeveloped.

14. K. Marx and F. Engels, *The German Ideology*, see Bottomore and Rubel, p.90

15. K. Marx and F. Engels, *The German Ideology*, Progress Publications 1964, p.21

16. J. Townsend, *A Dissertation on the Poor Laws*, by a Well-wisher of Mankind (1817), in *Capital*, 715, quoted by K. Popper, *The Open Society and its Enemies*, Routledge & Kegan Paul 1952, Vol. II, p.200

17. K. Marx, *Manuscripts of 1844*, quoted in D. B. McKown, op. cit., p.34

18. K. Marx, *Early Philosophical Manuscripts*, quoted in Bottomore and Rubel, p.251

19. D. B. McKown, op. cit., p.23

20. K. Marx and F. Engels, *Communist Manifesto* (1848), Section II. See *Essential Works of Marxism*, ed. A. P. Mendel, Bantam Books 1965, pp.25ff.

21. K. Popper, *The Open Society and its Enemies*, Vol. II, p.85

22. See below p.70f.

23. K. Marx, *Capital* I ET, Foreign Languages Publishing House, Moscow, p.593, note.

24. See, for example, the classic study of 1911 by E. Troeltsch, *The Social Teaching of the Christian Churches*, ET, Allen & Unwin 1956, pp.1004ff.

25. As samples, see statements issued by the World Council of Churches; the documents of the Second Vatican Council; the works of 'Liberation Theologians' such as G. Gutierrez, J. Miguez Bonino from South America, James Cone from the USA, J. Metz from Europe.

26. Quoted in J. M. Bonino, *Christians and Marxists*, Hodder & Stoughton 1976, p.17

27. K. Popper, *The Open Society and its Enemies*, Vol. II, pp.200f.

28. K. Marx, *The Critique of the Gotha Programme* (1875), quoted in Bottomore and Rubel, p.263

29. See *Essential Works of Marxism*, ed. A. P. Mendel, pp.420ff.

30. Carl E. Braaten, 'Toward a Theology of Hope', in *New Theology*, no.5, ed. D. Peerman and M. Marty, Macmillan 1965, p.99

31. See Carl E. Braaten, 'Toward a Theology of Hope', p.106

1. *Division of Labour* (1893); *Rules of Sociological Method* (1895); *Suicide* (1897)

2. Emile Durkheim, *The Elementary Forms of the Religious Life*, (1912), ET, J. W. Swain, first published 1915, second edition, Allen & Unwin 1976

3. See articles in W. S. F. Pickering (ed.), *Durkheim on Religion*, Routledge & Kegan Paul 1975

4. See note 8, p.83 above

5. Robert Bierstedt, *Emile Durkheim*, Weidenfeld & Nicolson 1969, p.205

6. I. M. Lewis, quoted in W. S. F. Pickering (ed.), *Durkheim on Religion*, p.4

7. Emile Durkheim, *Elementary Forms,*, p.70

8. Ibid., p.417

9. Ibid., p.70

10. Ibid., pp.2f.

11. Ibid., p.188

12. Ibid., pp.206f.

13. Ibid., p.47

14. Ibid., p.44

15. Ibid., p.9

16. Ibid., p.10

17. Ibid., p.429

18. Ibid., p.419

19. Ibid., p.416

20. Ibid., pp.416f.

21. Ibid., p.382

22. Ibid., p.431

23. Ibid., p.427

24. Ibid., pp.427f.

25. Ibid., p. 431

26. R. A. Nisbet, *Emile Durkheim*, Prentice-Hall 1965, p.74.

27. G. Radcliffe Brown, one of Durkheim's admirers, found as regards method Durkheim's interpretation of Australian totemism seriously defective.

28. See above p.68

29. Max Weber, *The Protestant Ethic and the Spirit of Capitalism*, Scribner 1958. See R. Aron, *Main Currents in Sociological Thought*, Vol. 2, Penguin Books 1977, pp.217f.

30. Emile Durkheim, *Elementary Forms*, p.422

31. R. Aron, *Main Currents in Sociological Thought*, Vol. 2, p.68

32. S. Kierkegaard, in *Fear and Trembling*, Doubleday, pp.70, 82, 89 and 102

33. A. N. Whitehead, *Religion in the Making*, World Publishing Company 1969, p.16

34. Emile Durkheim, *Elementary Forms*, p.425

35. Ibid., p.426

36. M. J. Jackson, *The Sociology of Religion*, Batsford 1974

37. For two very different examples, see J. McIntyre, *On the Love of God*, Collins 1962; and H. Richardson, *A Theology for the New World*, SCM Press 1968

38. See e.g., R. Gill, *Social Context of Theology*, Mowbray 1975

Postscript (pp.78–81)

1. A. J. Ayer, *Language, Truth and Logic*, Victor Gollancz 1936, Penguin Books 1971

2. A good summary of the discussion it initiated in theology is Frederick Ferré, *Language, Logic and God*, Harper & Row 1961